D1563556

Almost a Famous Person

Herb Michelson

Almost
a Famous
Person

Harcourt Brace Jovanovich
New York and London

Requests for permission to make copies of
any part of the work should be mailed to:
Permissions, Harcourt Brace Jovanovich, Inc.
757 Third Avenue, New York, N.Y. 10017

Set in Linotype Bodoni

Printed in the United States of America

Library of Congress Cataloging in Publication Data
Michelson, Herb.
Almost a famous person.
1. Presley, Bob, 1946–1975.
2. Basketball players—United States—Biography.
I. Title.
GV884.P73M5   796.32′3′0924   [B]   79-2766
ISBN 0-15-105069-4

First edition

B C D E

Almost a Famous Person

Prologue

Bob Presley stood, dazed, at the corner of Alberta and Minnesota streets in Portland, Oregon, early on the cloudy, chilly morning of Tuesday, March 25, 1975. Portland always seemed a gray place.

He had told the white family with whom he'd crashed during the night to drop him off near the freeway. He said he was thinking of thumbing back to Oakland. Now he was on a concrete bridge overlooking a green highway sign: "Fwy South 5." Oakland was six, seven hundred miles down that road, and if he was going back, he'd have to thumb because the paycheck he'd cashed last Friday from Scotlan's was nearly wiped out. Five days had gone just like that; he could barely remember any of them, except maybe Sunday when he'd messed up trying to see Bill Russell in the locker room in Seattle.

He walked to the other side of the bridge, past the entrance ramp to the freeway at Minnesota Street, and continued along Alberta. There was too much commuter traffic down there to thumb now. Nobody would stop for a big black guy anyway.

Three blocks west on Alberta, he saw Christ's Grocery at the stoplighted intersection with Interstate Avenue. With his last twenty-dollar bill he bought a Coke and a package of chocolate doughnuts. He borrowed a pencil from the clerk, tore a blank page out of his address book, and wrote, "Need new address." He was getting organized.

Bob asked the clerk for directions to the Trailblazers' arena and then headed down Interstate Avenue toward the Memorial Coliseum, intending to ask the team's general manager, Stu Inman, for a tryout. Bob's minor league coach had told him Inman might take a look at him. Bill Walton was giving the Blazers trouble; they could use a big man like Bob Presley.

Bob cut across the empty Coliseum parking lot and followed signs down a long flight of stairs to a stretch of glass doorways labeled "Arena." He tried one door. Locked. Then four more. All locked. He knew he should have called Inman first. He was too early, and too late. Portland was out, and Seattle. And Oakland and Detroit.

Without knowing or caring where he walked, Bob zigzagged through a maze of dead-end streets and finally wound up on busy Union Avenue, on the east side of the Willamette River, past a series of bridge accesses. He had never seen a town with so many bridges. At a 76 gas station at Burnside and Union he bought another Coke and stood watching commuters head up toward the Burnside Bridge. People with something to do.

Six blocks away, on the Union Avenue walkway under the Morrison Bridge, he sat down to rest, using his bag as a seat. He was briefly fascinated by the surrealistic patterns of the supports, pilings, moorings, and girders under the Morrison. Another damned bridge. Only Olympic swimmers could get around in this damned town, and here he was not able to swim at all.

Bob thought about Lake Merritt in Oakland, about the day his Cal teammate and good friend Waddell Blackwell coaxed him into renting a canoe on Merritt. Waddell put him at such ease that Bob enjoyed the canoe ride. The very next day he took Rae canoeing. But this time he relaxed too much, and the canoe tipped. Bob didn't remember much after he went into the water, except that Rae kept grabbing at him and yelling, "Hold on, turkey. Damn it, hold onto me." They had to get a rescue squad to drag him out.

Rae. She'd done everything for him a woman could. But now Rae was out, too.

A few more blocks of walking brought Bob to Water Street, just under the Hawthorne Bridge. He set his bag down on a dirt traffic island, unzipped it, took off his warmup jacket, and put it in the bag. From his address book he tore out the page with the listing of his minor league coach, folded the page, and put it into a trouser pocket. Organized.

Bob left the bag behind and walked up a dirt pathway leading to the bridge. He sprinted across Main Street, through a gap in the traffic, and onto the walkway on the north side of the Hawthorne. The traffic buzzed over the steel grating of the bridge ramp and made the walkway shudder.

The Portland skyline was directly in front of him. Down below, to the right, Bob saw several uniformed men lounging in front of Engine 7 Boat Station of the Portland Fire Department.

He didn't have to walk out too far. He was high enough. He was pleased that he had figured it out.

He paused at light pole number forty-five on the Hawthorne Bridge, climbed over the gray, cross-hatched metal railing, nudged himself backward, and slipped far down into the Willamette River.

1

ALL THE FAMILIES were large. Bob was the middle child of seven. His father, Robert Lewis Presley, was the youngest of seven, and his mother, Edna Johnson Presley, was the third of six. The height was in her family. From her Bob drew his size and sense of humor. From his father came the solitude.

Edna and Robert were both Alabamians. Robert's paternal grandparents had come from someplace in Texas, and no one ever told him about his mother's family. In fact, all four of his grandparents died at early ages, and he never recalled seeing any of them.

Robert Lewis Presley was born in 1919 in the east central Alabama town of Lafayette, whose population of some two thousand was almost entirely rural, dependent on the yield of the cotton, corn, and peanut crops and the graciousness of the white landowners who sliced their fields into tenant farms. Robert's father, Ora Presley, rented about one hundred acres at High Pine from Henry Tucker; the annual rent was one bale of cotton for each twenty acres. Ora had two horses, six reluctant mules, and all seven of his children working for him. By the time Robert took his place in the fields, at the age of nine, most of his brothers and sisters had married and moved away from Lafayette to farms elsewhere. One brother, Victor, gave up farming completely and went to work in a sawmill there in Chambers County. Victor, the family's man on the move, eventually lured brother Robert to Detroit.

The Presley boys did not go to school beyond the seventh or eighth grade, and the school they did attend, run by Mister Tucker for his farm families, always released the youngsters to work in the fields in early spring anyway. The combination of ample rainfall, fertile soil, and moderate average temperatures gave that patch of Alabama a long growing season of more than two hundred days. The workday during planting and harvesting times was sunup to sundown, and until Robert reached his teens, he was not paid by his father, who told him that food and a place to sleep were wages enough. Robert helped clear the land, cutting and raking and burning brush in the spring and then cutting the cotton stalks in the late summer. By the end of a September, Ora Presley sold his cotton for between sixty and eighty dollars a bale and paid off his kin hands with clothing. One season Robert received a cap and slippers.

There were white hands in the fields in Chambers County, and Robert mingled with some of them at High Pine and in swimming holes. "But when a white boy got to be twenty-one, we couldn't play with them no more. We had to say 'Yes, sir' and 'No, sir' to them then. We talked, but we weren't together anymore."

When Robert was eleven, he met Edna Johnson at the Mount Olive Baptist Church, ten miles south in Waverly. Edna was seven. The Johnson family had just moved down from Anniston expecting more money in Waverly, where Edna's paternal grandfather, Alfred Johnson, not only worked a seventy-five-acre farm but actually owned his own land. Johnson had told his son Claude that if he'd move to Waverly, he'd build him a house and give him plenty of work.

In Anniston, a rail junction, Claude had unloaded freight cars; Edna's mother, Sarah Finch Johnson, spent her time on the fringe of railroading as a cook and laundress at a workers' camp. The Johnsons, eight of them, had rented a two-bedroom house in Anniston. The crowding was such that Edna's brother, Osie, moved in with his Grandma Finch for nearly ten years. The prospect of a new house and new work in Waverly was more than attractive to Claude Johnson.

Waverly was a Negro settlement of about two hundred people. Seeing a white person away from the fields was an occasion for Edna, and although the Ku Klux Klan was active in Alabama in the 1920s, its activities were not visible in Chambers County.

Edna was told that her Grandpa Johnson had come to Chambers County from Abilene, Texas, with a white family. He was "a blue-eyed, half-white nigger," she said, but she never learned the origins of those blue eyes. He built her family a small house just behind his own home and gave Claude plenty of work. Grandpa Johnson often hired out the kids to white farmers; Edna was awakened by her mother at dawn and handed a ten-gallon pail containing biscuits and a jug of syrup and then another pail with milk. Her father took her to the fields in a mule-drawn wagon, every day, sun to sun, from April through June, with a pause only for lunch out of the pails. After planting, there was some time off starting around the Fourth of July. Then back to harvesting.

The white farmers paid their Negro pickers seventy-five cents per hundred pounds of cotton, but Edna never could seem to surpass thirty-five pounds in a day. True, she was a large girl for her age, usually the biggest in her class at school, but the stooping got to her. Ethel, her oldest sister, was also quite tall and could pick nearly two hundred pounds in a day's shift.

Edna's mother didn't have to work outside the property in Waverly. She did spend some time in her father-in-law's fields, but at least there was food available there and in a garden on the Johnson land. After she did the slaughtering, the family ate plenty of chicken, turkey, and ham, topped with what was called thicklin' gravy, a mixture of flour and grease.

The social life in the area revolved around the Mount Olive Baptist Church, the locus for the Negroes of Chambers County. The Johnson and Presley families went to Mount Olive as often as three nights a week. During revival time there were processions from church to church throughout the county. All the "socials" were church-centered: dances, games, box suppers, covered-dish dinners. "There wasn't anything else to do," said Edna, "but I loved it. When we had to stay home and work and couldn't go to church, I felt really bad because that was the only place we had. That was our whole life. That was all we saw: the fields and the house and the church. I never did see anything better than that then. I didn't know there was anything else out there. I didn't dream about anything big because I didn't know what you were supposed to dream about. People ask me if we were all kinda hopeless in those days. Seems like we should have been, I guess, but we weren't because we never did see any better than what we had."

The Johnsons' only luxury was an old record player Claude had scrounged. There was one record to play on it: "Casey Jones."

At Titanic School, just outside Waverly, Edna and her sisters were called "those Johnson girls—they're so big that if you don't get them first, they're sure to get you." Only Mother Sarah Johnson was short, five-two. Father Claude was just over six feet tall. The only son, Osie, was six-four. Ethel, the oldest sister, reached six-one. The two youngest girls, Lucille and Lorraine, grew to five-nine and five-eleven. And by the time Edna was out of her teens she was nearly six-three. By then she was married and had two children and was about three inches taller than her husband.

When they were youngsters in Chambers County there was little time, and less energy, for sports. Robert occasionally played a little pickup baseball in a pasture with his future brother-in-law Osie, and Edna shot baskets in the schoolyard with a few of the girls during recesses at Titanic. But because she was the tallest girl in class, and had been since kindergarten, the other young ladies eventually made it known that they didn't want Edna on the court with them. She was too tall and too good, and she understood their point of view—it just wasn't fair for her to compete against them. She laughed off this banishment, but later she saw it as the first gesture of size discrimination against her.

Not until graduation from Titanic and passage up to high school in Lafayette did size bother Edna. At Lafayette High School she suddenly found herself a contemporary of girls with pretty dresses and pretty shoes. The dresses were not so intimidating. Lafayette required a semblance of a uniform for its female students: blue dresses. Sarah made two for Edna and washed and starched and ironed them every other day to keep her daughter from looking shabby. Shoes and socks were another matter. Most of the other girls had several pairs of shoes and a variety of stockings, but Edna had trouble with shoes. Her feet grew so quickly she was never sure of her size; her feet were big, unfeminine, awkward. Just finding shoes to fit was a problem. Sarah worked overtime in the fields picking cotton to get a little extra money to buy new shoes and socks for Edna, but still the girl kept outgrowing her footwear.

Edna enjoyed Titanic because three of her father's cousins taught there. Claude Johnson was one of thirteen children, and his brothers and sisters had raised three preachers and four teachers, several of whom had even attended college. Not that Edna expected to go to college herself. She expected to follow the natural course of a young woman in Waverly: work on the family farm until the end of high school, then marry and have children and help a husband on his tenant acreage. That's how it was. Edna expected no different.

Edna's size made her different from the other girls. Her closest friend at Titanic was a plump girl named Mattie McCurdy. Some of the other students called them "the Pig and the Camel." One day, when Edna was fourteen, she challenged a name-caller to a fight. The long-limbed "Camel" jumped the girl, threw punches, pulled hair, choked—and Edna was suspended from school for three days. She thought that was unfair "because I didn't hurt the girl that bad." But from then on, nobody in Waverly or Lafayette ever called Edna names.

After Robert Presley dropped out of school in the seventh grade, he still farmed his father's land. Robert decided his father could be more successful if he saved money and leased more land from Mister Tucker. He thought his dad "frolicked up" his money: other women, an investment in bootlegging. Ora had built a large still behind his property and worked it about six months a year, producing a sizable quantity of good corn liquor for himself, his relatives, and neighbors. The still held a batch of one hundred pounds of sugar and an equal amount of corn; from this mix came nearly twenty gallons of whiskey. When he was still a boy, Robert stood guard duty at the edge of the woods near the still. Later, he sold it and drank it.

Robert expected to stay on the farm. He assumed his father would eventually sublet some of his acreage to him. He also assumed that he would eventually marry Edna Johnson; they were waiting to reach what was considered the proper age and the proper circumstances to marry. "There was nothing else to do when you were sixteen or seventeen except to get married," said Edna. "If you didn't do that, you just had to work in the fields." Edna thought about waiting a few more years but was fearful that, because of her size, no other man would be interested. She had no self-confidence about her physical appearance and was amazed when, some fifteen years later, she discovered that many men considered her to be terribly attractive. But Edna Johnson chose the prudent, practical course: grab a man if he's ready to grab you. Which Robert Presley was.

"I was worried that maybe somebody else would get Edna if I waited longer," he said. "I didn't have any set plans in mind except to work and get married. I just wanted a job, and I just wanted a wife like Edna. No big dreams. No thinking about saving money before you got married. You couldn't wait until you saved 'cause there was no money to be saved."

The same thought, with a different conclusion, occurred to Edna's father. Claude Johnson felt that Robert

Presley couldn't support Edna and worried that he would have to provide for the young couple. Sarah told her husband there was no reason to object to the marriage, and Edna told her dad she was more than ready. But Claude sulked and on the wedding day didn't even come to the ceremony, which was held in his own home. Several hours after the wedding, he stopped by the house to tell Edna not to worry. If she and Robert ever needed help, he would give them a dollar or a biscuit, he said; if Edna had to move back home for any reason, she would be welcomed.

There was no honeymoon. "Who knew about honeymoons?" wondered Edna. "They may have been going on, but I sure never heard about them."

They went up the ten miles to Lafayette, where Ora Presley had built his son and new daughter-in-law a two-room shack on his tenant land as a wedding present. The place had a kitchen, a sleeping room, and an adjacent outhouse. The morning after the wedding, both Robert and Edna began clearing the twenty acres Ora had sublet to his son under the same arrangement the father had with Mister Tucker: a bale of cotton annually for rent. Edna had a new name and the same old life.

Their first child, McLister, was prompt. The wedding had been on February 17, 1940, and McLister was born November 17, 1940, the first of seven children over seventeen years. Only McLister was born in Chambers County.

Robert was scratching on his farmland there. He felt he'd made a sucker deal with his father. There was little money left for anything else after paying the bale for rent. But Robert was also frolicking, not tending his crops as he should have, driving around with his infant son in a 1929 Chevrolet purchased soon after the marriage. "Me and McLister just drove about seeing the world," he said. But driving soon became as tedious as the farming, and in 1942, with Edna again pregnant, Robert went northwest to Birmingham. There was money to be made in the new industrial complex there, even by a young Negro.

"I was tired of farming," Robert explained. "I was tired of working for my father. When I was out driving on the highway with McLister in my lap, I always thought about how I could get away from the farm."

Military service would have been a possibility, but Robert had knee troubles and was given a physical discharge one week after he was drafted into the army. And so Birmingham was the answer, for Edna too.

"The farm life was not the thing either one of us wanted to do," she said. "I didn't appreciate having to work while I was pregnant. Having to hoe corn and stoop to pick cotton. And we never did see any money off that farm either."

For the first time in her life, Edna had a goal: a house. A big house. A real house. Birmingham might be the source of money for that house. At night she fantasized about a home they owned on land they owned. Robert listened and nodded and let her aspire; eventually Edna would conclude that there was no way they would ever have enough money to buy the kind of house she wanted. Robert didn't disagree.

His first job in Birmingham, as a grinder at a stove-manufacturing company, paid thirty cents an hour. The Presleys rented an apartment at forty-five dollars a month but left it after only a few weeks when neighbors objected to McLister's crying. Next they rented a small one-bedroom house at the same price, but with indoor plumbing. For Edna, this was civilization. She discovered the existence of grits and, more intimidating, the necessity to pay money for such staples as food. In Waverly and Lafayette there had been gardens and live-stock. In Birmingham there were grocery stores. For a woman not yet twenty who had rarely seen cash, this business of not only carrying around money but actually handing it over to strangers was cause for deep insecur-ity. More than once she asked Robert to take her back home.

But within a few months he left the stove company for an assembly line job at a pipe foundry, at double his previous wage. Seventy cents an hour looked very good to Robert—until Margie was born late in 1942, and Maxine in 1944, and Nathaniel Robert Presley in 1946. So Robert found odd jobs and weekend jobs. He put in his shift at the pipe foundry, then drove a truck, then caught on at the Birmingham railroad station as a bag-gage handler.

But after the war ended, he was laid off at the foundry and couldn't find full-time work anywhere else. In 1946 the rent increased, as did the electricity bill. And the house on Twenty-third Street was packed with people: Margie and Maxine slept in the kitchen; McLister was on a couch in the middle of the Presleys' bedroom, sharing space with a coal heater.

"It was hard times then," said Edna. "I never got so hungry in my life. Once my brother Osie stopped by to see us while he was on leave from the army and gave us twenty dollars so we could get some food. But still we like to starve to death. I said to myself that if I had the baby I was carrying and I didn't die when I had it, I would get a job. We couldn't afford another child. I knew that. And abortions were only for the rich."

2

THE CLINIC listed Edna's second son as Robert Nathaniel Presley. The name was to be Nathaniel Robert, but somebody got confused. Edna had picked Nathaniel because she'd heard a boy by that name being cheered in a baseball game in a park one day. She didn't want two Roberts in the family; neither did her husband. They always called their second son Nathaniel.

At birth, April 30, 1946, he weighed nine pounds and measured thirty inches in length. The nurses who came into Edna's room kept telling her, "He be so long."

Edna went to work soon after Nathaniel's birth. She took a job as a maid at Methodist Hospital on the 7:00 A.M. shift. Her husband had just found a full-time job at U.S. Steel on a shift that began at 4:00 P.M.

They developed a routine: Edna made breakfast and went to work, waking her husband before she left the house. He took care of the children—baby-sitting and making them lunch. Just after three o'clock, he left the house and went to work himself. They met at the bus

17

stop, quickly exchanged news about the children, and then headed their separate ways, Edna going home to make supper.

The two jobs permitted them to survive financially for a few years, at least until their fifth child, Marilyn, was born in 1949. Edna had to quit her job then, and Robert wasn't picking up sufficient hours at the steel plant to compensate. Once again there wasn't enough money for food for the seven people now in the house on Twenty-third Street. Robert told Edna, "Anything has to be better than Birmingham." She agreed.

Robert's older brother Victor had a good job at U.S. Rubber in Detroit. The Motor City was thriving in the postwar boom, and it occurred to Robert—just as when he'd left Lafayette for Birmingham—that a move to a bigger city might lead to a few more dollars and at least a partial sense of security. He was tired of treadmilling in Birmingham. He knew, as did Edna, that there were times he didn't push hard enough for more and higher-paying work there. She often accused him of "piddlin' around." But in his way he tried to be responsible. Perhaps it would be easier to be responsible in Detroit, and he wrote to Victor asking for help in finding a job up there.

"Catch the next thing smokin'," Victor quickly wrote back, and Robert was immediately off for the biggest city he had ever seen in his twenty-nine years. Within two weeks he had a job at U.S. Rubber. "This is the most beautifulest place in the world," he wrote Edna.

She sold the few pieces of furniture they owned and in September 1950 put herself and the five children on a train for Detroit. "Anything will beat this place," she told a neighbor in parting. "I'm so glad to get away from here." She packed only a pillow, a hammer, and an iron.

But the living quarters awaiting the Presley family in Detroit were worse than those she'd left behind—Robert had decided to accept his brother's offer to stay at his house for fifteen dollars a month plus a share of the utility costs. Victor and Laura Presley and their five children had a two-story home with two bedrooms, one bathroom, and a kitchen on the first floor and a large, bare attic on the second. The seven Birmingham Presleys slept on the floor of the attic, and soon after Edna moved in, she had the distinct impression her sister-in-law was not overjoyed with the living arrangements. Edna couldn't blame her; she was even less delighted.

Every time one of Edna's children wanted to use the bathroom, one of Laura's children was in it, and so Edna put a "slop jar" in the attic. The families ate separately. Edna was allowed to cook from seven to seven thirty each morning and from two thirty to three every afternoon. "But by the time I pulled out a skillet and struck a match to light the stove, Laura'd be ready to cook herself," said Edna.

"Lord," she sobbed on the phone to her mother, "I am throwed away now. And this time I'm so far away from home. At the road's end."

In the first few months in Detroit, Edna received small amounts of money from her mother and her brother and secondhand clothing from her sister Ethel. But what she most wanted, more than the money, was a place of her own. When Edna gave birth to Melinda late in 1950, it meant fifteen people sharing a small house—that made for hostility, not hospitality, and so Edna pleaded with Robert to find another place for them to live.

Every day after work Robert walked around Victor's neighborhood and other areas looking for a rental. "I'll show you," he told Edna. "We gonna do better. I'm gonna be findin' us a house." He took Edna for bus rides through more attractive neighborhoods and pointed out houses he knew she liked, houses both knew they could not afford even though Robert was now also working weekends as a truck loader.

Money wasn't the only problem. They also had to find a landlord who would rent to a family with six children. Finally, in March 1951, after Robert left U.S. Rubber for a job as a maintenance man at Ford Motor Company, the Presleys found the right house.

But, as it turned out, it was owned by the wrong landlord.

A friend at Ford tipped off Robert about a small house being vacated that very night on Luddington Street in suburban Inkster. The rental agent had orders not to rent to families with children, but he was malleable, fifty dollars' worth of malleable. Robert paid him off and, ordering the children to hush, moved his family in just before midnight. The landlord came around the next morning, though, suspicious, wondering what had become of the former tenants. Edna lied, telling him the old tenants had asked her to tend the place while they were on vacation for a few weeks. He believed her for another day, until a nearby tenant snitched about the six children. Next morning the landlord told Edna she'd have to move within twenty-four hours. She cried. Every morning for six months when the landlord came to evict her, she cried, asking for one more day, one more day to find another place. He ultimately set a deadline of October 1. "If you aren't out of here by then, I'll bring a wheelbarrow and haul your furniture out to the street," he said. Edna didn't tell him she had no furniture.

The only solution was to buy a house, but there wasn't enough money for a down payment.

Robert was now working full-time on the assembly line at Ford, picking up overtime shifts, too. He was earning enough to put food on the table, pay the rent, and buy his children two pairs of shoes each—one for everyday wear, one for Sunday. But he could no more buy a house than he could buy the Ford Motor Company.

Not until Edna got lucky. Very, very lucky.

Edna spent the summer evenings of 1951 sitting on the steps of her little house in the project in Inkster. Chatting with neighbors. Trying to keep cool. One of the neighbors, a woman Edna knew only as Margaret, was always talking about "the night number." Edna had no idea what she meant.

"You don't play the numbers, do you?" Margaret said.

"No, honey, what's that?" asked Edna, who had heard about the numbers in Birmingham but wasn't sure what they were. "How do you play?"

"You have to dream," Margaret said. "Just go to sleep and dream, and then come over here in the morning and tell me about your dream and give me some money, and I'll give you a number to play."

Edna said, "But I don't never dream, honey."

"Try," said Margaret. "Try, and you might make some money." And Margaret showed Edna a small book, a kind of dictionary in which hundreds of words were listed with corresponding numbers. Not definitions. Numbers.

"Whatever you dream about has a number," said Margaret, "so go to sleep and dream."

Edna wasn't able to dream the first few nights after Margaret's explanation. But she gave Margaret a nickel in the morning anyway and picked out any old number, with no success. Then one night in September, Edna dreamed about her sister Ethel. When she awakened, she couldn't wait to hurry over and get a numerical translation from Margaret.

The word *sister* was listed in Margaret's book as number 252. Edna gave her a dime, which Margaret added to the neighborhood collection to be turned over to her husband, the local numbers runner. But 252 didn't hit that night.

Once more Edna dreamed of Ethel. Once more she played 252, this time with a twenty-five-cent wager. And this time Edna did hit—for one hundred dollars.

But Edna was just warming up.

Three nights later, she dreamed of her father; Claude Johnson had died a few years earlier after separating from his wife. Again, Edna asked Margaret for a number that represented the dream. Margaret flipped through the book and stopped at number 769, which translated to "the dead man."

Edna bet fifty cents on 769. And won five hundred dollars.

"I don't believe it," said Margaret.

"*You* don't believe it?" said Edna. "There won't be nobody believe this."

"Tell 'em all anyway," laughed Margaret. "Tell 'em all, girl, and give my collection a big name."

The Presleys now were within sight of having enough money for a down payment on a house Robert had seen on Delmar Avenue on the north side of Detroit. Two sisters owned the house and were interested in selling, although one of the elderly women wanted to stay on and rent the rear portion of the house. Robert borrowed one hundred dollars from the Ford credit union. Added to Edna's numbers winnings, the total was almost enough to make the purchase. It was necessary to take a second mortgage for the balance, but in the face of their pending eviction from Inkster, Edna and Robert were willing to contend with the problem of high monthly payments. They closed the deal. Edna Johnson Presley finally had a home of her own.

Nathaniel Robert was only five years old when the Presleys moved to Delmar Avenue. He was an unobtrusive child, lost in the shuffle of a household with six children, a working mother, and a working father. He was not particularly close to his only brother. He was not particularly close to any member of his family. He went to Maybee Elementary School; he carried out his only assigned household chore, emptying the garbage; he was just there. His only distinction as the years went along was his size. When he was noticed by family and neighbors, it was because he stood above family and neighbors. The kids at school started calling him "Treetop."

Nathaniel hated that nickname.

To help meet the house payments, $110 a month, Edna went back to work early in 1952. Until that time she was afraid to venture alone outside her block. Robert did most of the shopping and even went downtown to the department stores to buy her underwear. Edna was frightened and reclusive. But with all the bills to pay and furniture to buy, it made no sense to her to stay in the house all day. She also felt confined.

The place on Delmar had two bedrooms, a kitchen, living room, one bath, and, that familiar territory, an attic. Edna and Robert had a bedroom to themselves; McLister and Nathaniel shared the other; the four girls were in the attic.

The oldest girls, Margie, nearly ten, and Maxine, almost eight, could relieve Edna of the housecleaning work. Robert was on the night shift at Ford and didn't object to doing the cooking, so Edna realized she could be spared. Her experience at the hospital in Birmingham helped her get a job as a maid at the Community Nursing Home in Detroit at fifty-two cents an hour, just over five dollars a day.

Except for a break in 1957 to give birth to her seventh, and final, child, Denise, she worked at Community steadily for the next eight years. By the time she quit in 1960, she had been promoted to second cook and raised in pay to six dollars a day. During those years, Edna Presley turned into something of a swinger.

She rarely saw her husband; Edna got the breakfast and the kids started every morning and then took the bus to the hospital on Grand Boulevard. Robert awakened, hustled the older children off to school, and stayed home and watched the younger ones until it was time for him to leave for the Ford plant in late afternoon. There was plenty of overtime offered at the plant, so he usually was away from the house on weekends. Robert had neither the time nor the inclination to discipline the children; that burden was left to Edna. But Edna had less and less time herself. She discovered frolicking.

Edna was close with another maid, Johnnie Mae, at Community. Height may have been the attraction: Johnnie Mae was five-eleven. Johnnie Mae also was single and a night person. She was always urging Edna to join her for a few drinks after their shift at the hospital; Edna kept begging off. It wasn't that she didn't want to go out with Johnnie Mae and meet some people, but she was uncomfortable about the way she looked and dressed. Her wardrobe was limited and ill-fitting. She was ashamed to be seen in public in the skimpy clothing she owned. She could hardly wear a short, faded housedress while stepping out with Johnnie Mae, and the only dresses Edna had that fit were two white hospital uniforms a seamstress had made for her. They were fine for work, but for work only. "I want to be and go like the rest of the people," Edna told Johnnie Mae, "but I can't."

After the birth of Denise, Edna finally decided to make an effort. She was tired of looking drab. She was weary of her work and of the family. She was exhausted with pinching pennies. If there wasn't anguish about paying bills, there was some other problem.

McLister, for one.

Her oldest son was giving her trouble. He wouldn't go to school. He had often skipped grade school classes and now wasn't showing up at all at Sherrard Junior High. The Presleys' neighborhood was rife with incidents of drug use, and Edna and Robert weren't sure what McLister was up to. They decided that McLister should leave Detroit, and so in 1957, when he was seventeen, McLister enlisted in the army. For Edna that year it was one child in, one child out. And time to take care of herself.

Edna went shopping in downtown Detroit at the big department stores, a woman of thirty-five years on a clothes-buying spree for the first time in her life. Except that she couldn't find anything in her size without a fifty-dollar price tag. Then Johnnie Mae told her about a sale on extra-long sizes at Lane Bryant. In a good dress, a dress that fit, Edna was dazzling.

When she started making the rounds of various bars and clubs with Johnnie Mae after work, she noticed that people, particularly men, looked at her more than routinely. "Probably because I'm so tall," she said to Johnnie Mae at first. But the men who approached her did not mention her height; they did not discuss six-three; they mentioned beauty.

"I began to think I was the prettiest thing there ever was," said Edna. "I was just the finest lady who ever walked in any club anywhere."

The club Johnnie Mae and Edna settled on was the Picket Fence, a spot with a bar and dance floor in Edna's own neighborhood. The two tall women were regulars. Night after night after work.

Even when Edna quit Community in 1960 to take a job at the Whittier Nursing Home as first cook for eight dollars a day, she continued to play with Johnnie Mae and the gentlemen who frequented the Picket Fence. Edna didn't worry about her children; Robert was now on the day shift at Ford and staying home with the children in the evenings. Or so Edna thought.

On one of the rare nights she was home, Robert excused himself and said he was going out for a barbecue and a Coke. He didn't come back for a week; Robert had other friends, too. He was tired of working and tending children, too. Robert had not forgotten how to frolic.

A few days before her fortieth birthday in 1963, Edna received an invitation from Johnnie Mae for a big, cele-bratory night on the town. Edna phoned back. "I'm tired, girl. I'm not goin' no more." And she stopped.

The marriage held together from then on with less strain and more contact than it had in the previous five years. Robert and Edna finally were too tired to think about being too tired.

3

IN THE FIRST five and one-half years of his life, Nathaniel Presley lived in four different homes. Whenever he talked about his childhood, in rare conversations with friends in Berkeley and Oakland and San Francisco, he talked in negatives.

Much of the time as a child he was hungry. There was food on the Presley table, but never quite enough for the appetite of a boy who seemed to grow daily in height and weight.

He had clothing, but his trousers never reached his ankles. The cuffs of his shirts stretched down only to mid-forearm. His socks and shoes were too tight, so it was often painful to walk. He tried unlacing the shoes, stretching the backs with his hands, but usually he'd end up sort of half in and half out of a pair. And when he did get a pair of new shoes, they'd quickly be outgrown.

Nathaniel was frustrated that he couldn't keep up with himself. He was uncomfortable about the way he looked. The other boys he knew around Delmar Avenue weren't fancy dressers, but their clothing fit, their shoes were laced, their sleeves and cuffs were long enough.

He was different. Not richer or poorer, or smarter or dumber, or faster or slower. Bigger. He wondered if he fit, and where. But neither his sisters nor his brother received any more, or less, attention at home. None got more to eat or more clothing or more space or more of Robert and Edna's time. Silence and solitude offered him refuge. Nathaniel discovered early that he was happier, or at least more comfortable, when he was alone.

Outside the family he felt better; he felt freer. Outside he was an individual. There were opportunities; he didn't feel locked in, clamped by hunger, cramped by inattention. And there was a lot to be said for those days and nights he worked at the store for Mister Curry.

Leonard (Butch) Curry ran the neighborhood grocery on Westminster, just around the corner from the Presley house. The grocery was a hangout for the kids of the neighborhood. Everybody knew the Currys, and the Currys knew everybody. Nathaniel always stopped by to listen and watch and ask Butch if there was anything for him to do.

The store was a family operation—at one time or another Butch's wife and daughter and two sons worked there—and Butch couldn't really afford to employ somebody whose name wasn't Curry. But he liked the Presley kid, thought him polite and willing. And so when Nathaniel was eleven and still courteously badgering Mister Curry for work, Butch let the boy come with him on his truck when he made deliveries or picked up produce. Before too long, Nathaniel was spending more time with the Currys than with the Presleys.

Depending on how good business was on a particular

day, Butch paid Nathaniel forty or fifty cents, or he let him take home a box of cookies and a couple of bottles of soda pop. Nathaniel didn't care if Butch gave him money. Keeping busy was more important than pay. Doing things on his own. And the nice thing about working for Mister Curry was the flexibility. If Nathaniel wanted to spend an afternoon in the alley behind his house shooting baskets with his friends, that was OK with Butch. Nathaniel could even sleep late on Saturdays and Sundays and not show up at Butch's until two or three in the afternoon. No matter. It was a job that wasn't a job, an alternative to boredom, a way to be on the streets without getting into trouble on the streets. And it was an entry into another family.

Nathaniel first got to know the Curry home because Butch sent him over to the house to feed his dog, a Belgian shepherd called Blue Boy: the first true love of Nathaniel's life. If he fed Blue Boy or gave him water or rubbed his neck, the dog turned over his soul to Nathaniel, a significant discovery for a lonely eleven-year-old.

The Presleys did not object to Nathaniel spending so much time at the grocery or at the Curry home. Robert and Edna always knew that if Nathaniel wasn't in his own house, he was with the Currys. Anyway, those were the days when Edna was either working or frolicking with Johnnie Mae. If Nathaniel was taking care of himself and staying out of trouble by hanging out with the Currys, that was OK with Edna. "It was someplace for him to be. Somethin' for him to do," she said.

Butch's daughter Rosemary was six years older than Nathaniel. She was married to a jazz musician, a bass player named Jones, and already had a child. She and her baby lived with Butch, who had also taken in his son's two small children. There was plenty of baby-sitting to be done at the Curry house, and Nathaniel either shared the job with Rosemary or, if she were needed at the grocery, watched all three of Butch's grandchildren himself.

"He got to be just like part of the family," said Rosemary. "That's how we looked on him, and I think that's how he saw us, too. We always tried to be loving people, to relate to everybody. So Nathaniel could relate to us. Maybe better than he related to his own people."

Nathaniel talked to Butch and Rosemary about things he had never discussed with his parents. He was more relaxed, more open with his second family—extraordinary for Nathaniel, who rarely said much of anything to anyone.

Nathaniel was at the Curry house so often, and with such easy intimacy, that Rosemary's husband began viewing the big kid as a threat—more as a man than a child. Still, he talked about jazz and musicians with Nathaniel, who suddenly showed an interest. Soon, he and several of his school friends began "playing" jazz as they walked in the neighborhood, clutching make-believe instruments, pretending they were plunking a bass, or sliding a trombone, or blowing a horn, making loud, not especially jazzlike noises. Along Delmar Avenue, you could hear Nathaniel and Bozie and Poochie coming before you saw them.

Butch Curry was the first businessman Nathaniel knew. While they rode in Curry's truck, the young man told his boss about his hopes for the future. Nathaniel said he'd like to go into business himself. "I want my own office," he said. "I can see myself sitting behind my own desk in my own office." He had no idea what kind of business he'd run from that desk in that office.

In Nathaniel's eyes, Butch was a successful business-man. And that's what he wanted for himself: success in some kind of business. Not necessarily a grocery store, but a business kind of business.

Nathaniel had grown up in an atmosphere of poverty. There wasn't enough money to go around and wouldn't be. He'd have to provide for himself, and to provide for himself it would be necessary to become successful. That was his answer. He would just do it, and, he hoped, suc-ceed as soon as possible. There was money to be made, somewhere.

Crime was one way. Every day on the streets Nathaniel heard about kids he knew who were involved with drugs or numbers or guns or prostitution or a combination of those activities. Because he was so tall for his age—at twelve, Nathaniel was already six-four—he was treated as a contemporary by several of the older guys in the neighborhood. He envied them their pocket money and flashy wardrobes. These people didn't have to ask any-body to buy them a pair of shoes.

"But I don't like trouble," he told Rosemary. "I'm not afraid, I don't think. I just got better things to think about and talk about. I wanna make my own plans and do things without trouble." He told her that guns and knives were tools of violence. "I don't want no trouble, and I don't want no violence," he said.

And Rosemary told him he was right to think that way.

School was dull. Nathaniel carefully listened to all of McLister's complaints about school. McLister often cut classes, and his mother argued with his brother about these absences. McLister had fled to the army rather than be bothered, but within six months he wrote home from

Germany asking his mother to get him a discharge. "I'm just a child, and I'm so far from home," McLister pleaded. "Please get me out of here."

And she did. Edna appealed to the Red Cross, which helped arrange his discharge on the basis of his being underage. But when McLister came home, he didn't return to school. There were immediate problems with dope, and soon the six-four, eighteen-year-old McLister was arrested. And it wasn't the only time. McLister's problems reinforced Nathaniel's conviction that trouble was really trouble; he wanted to help his brother, but he knew there was nothing a twelve-year-old could do, except try to stay out of trouble himself. The best way to stay out was to stay in school, yet he was bored with all of his classes because he was never sure what the teachers were talking about. He tried, but not too hard, to read the books and do the homework, but what he read and heard in school didn't make much sense to him. He was convinced he could learn more just by working for Butch Curry and listening to business conversations at the grocery. School was just school, where you always had to be on time.

Nathaniel never liked getting up in the mornings; he remained unaffected by life's insistence on punctuality. He would get there when he could get there—that was his notion. He talked to his mother about wanting to drop out of school after the eighth grade, and Edna gave him the same argument she'd always used with McLister: "You belong in school. You've got to keep going until you finish high school. That's what you're supposed to do, and that's what you're gonna do."

A few weeks before he was scheduled to graduate from Maybee and move on to Sherrard Junior High, Nathaniel told Edna he didn't intend to go to the graduation ceremony. He didn't tell her why, but she knew. It was the clothing.

She had been through the same insecurity of wearing clothes that didn't fit. She told Nathaniel she'd buy him new clothes for the graduation, but he laughed. "Clothes ain't no big thing," he said. Recently he had seen her searching through neighborhood garbage cans and watched as she pulled a pair of old shoes out of one. She had given him these shoes. He said nothing except "thanks," put the shoes in a closet, and never wore them.

But now at graduation time Edna wanted to do all she could for her younger son. She sensed an unhappy boy and thought that new clothes might help him just as they had helped her become more confident. She went to a men's big and tall clothing store and bought Nathaniel a shirt, pants, and a jacket. He had told her that many of the other kids had a watch, so she bought him one. But she couldn't find shoes to fit the diagram of his foot she'd outlined on a piece of newspaper. She gave him money and told him to buy his own shoes.

Edna watched him dress on graduation day. She walked to the school auditorium and sat down to view the ceremony. Whenever a name was called, that student walked up to the stage and got a diploma. When Nathaniel's name was called, however, he did not come to the stage. Edna wondered if it was his clothes.

But there was more bothering Nathaniel. Even in his early teens, he was a physically dominant figure in his neighborhood. One day Johnnie Mae drove Edna home from the hospital and asked her about the big guy standing on the corner near the grocery. Edna had to look twice to realize that Johnnie Mae was talking about her son. Edna couldn't keep up with Nathaniel.

"People are annoying me all the time coming up to my face and asking how tall I am," Nathaniel told his mother.

"I know what's bothering Nathaniel," Edna told Robert. "I know it because the same thing bothers me. But what can I do? What good is it to worry when there's nothin' you can do?"

Nathaniel continued to worry. When it was time to begin classes for his first year at Sherrard Junior High in the fall of 1960, he worried about all the new people he'd see, the new people looking at him. On the mornings he didn't sleep in, when he actually got up on time so that he could walk the few blocks to Sherrard and be prompt for his first class, he still cut. It was easier to pretend to go to school than to be badgered by Edna for not leaving the house. She always knew when he cut classes, even when he'd been at Maybee Elementary School. She'd see him on the street when he was supposed to be in school or someone she knew saw him and told her.

Nathaniel loved his mother, though, for caring. And helping his parents was important to him. More important than going to any school. And the best way to help them—Nathaniel's easy answer—was to play ball.

4

When Nathaniel was in the third grade at Maybee Elementary, the principal let him take an old, beat-up basketball that the school janitor was going to throw out. He and a friend managed to hang a net halfway up a telephone pole in the alley behind the house on Delmar. At first, they just banged the ball against the pole. Then they played one-on-one. Then enough other kids showed up for three-on-three games.

Basketball was easy for Nathaniel; he was so much taller than the others that he barely played. He just shot. No one was able to block him. He could hang under the hoop and score and score and score.

When he wasn't handling the big ball, he squeezed a little rubber ball—someone had told him that this was a good exercise for his wrists. And he read the sports pages. He was convinced that ball was the way out, the way to money and an office and a desk and success. It was all right there in the sports pages. Big men made big money. Simple.

The phrase "city game" was not yet a cliché when Nathaniel started playing ball. It took another half-dozen years for most fans of basketball to realize the full implications of the city game. And its sociology.

By now, less than two decades later, black athletes dominate basketball in both quantity and quality. Today, nearly every outstanding college basketball player is black. The overwhelming majority of professional basketball players are black. There has been a growing number of black assistant coaches and head coaches on both college and professional levels, and at least one professional team has employed a black as general manager.

Basketball has always been less structured than other major sports, more ramshackle, a transient riding the rails from concrete half courts on playgrounds to church gymnasiums to dimly lighted YMCA hardwoods to arenas of varying capacities and mixed architectural breeding. The game is big league but lacks the first-class facilities of other major sports, especially on the professional level.

An athlete steps up in class when he moves from the amateurs to the pros. This is not true in basketball, except on the salary level, where the average season's wage is approaching $90,000. In the National Basketball Association, players refuse to shower in some of the locker rooms; they return to their hotel rooms in sweaty uniforms to clean up. It is not uncommon to see large men in short pants walking into arena parking lots with towels shrouding their heads from the night air. And because pro teams must share arenas with a variety of other sports and entertainment events, it is not uncommon for a team playing in the championship round to have to scurry around for an alternate site and lose the home court advantage.

But there is money in pro hoops, and the money is the lure. The tall young men in the inner cities look at the sports pages, hear the radio, watch the TV, and understand the money. What they aren't informed about are the chances of success.

Less than 1 percent of the twenty-two thousand high school seniors playing basketball make it in the pros. Only sixty of each season's six thousand basketball-playing college seniors are signed by teams in the National Basketball Association. But all that the youngsters of the city game see is that "Tiny," an unprepossessing-looking athlete named Nate Archibald, is paid a half-million dollars to play eighty-two games of basketball for six months.

Detroit had produced its share of city game stars even before the colleges began to realize the value of employing tall, quick, young blacks to win them publicity and perhaps a championship or two. Detroit, in fact, gave more basketball players to the Harlem Globetrotters than Harlem or any other single city. But in the 1950s, and even early 1960s, the city's budding black players were generally anonymous, except to each other. They knew who could play, who could best "put the melon in the hole."

They came together at the gymnasium that served the Brewster public housing projects, Krink Recreation Center, or at the old auxiliary gymnasium at Wayne State University. There were big games at Brewster on Sundays. Games that drew a thousand spectators. Games

that went unreported in the *Free Press* and *News* because these were essentially pickup games; no leagues
or conferences or standings, just quality athletes.

In Nathaniel's time in Detroit, the most visible of the
city's ballplayers was a student at Eastern High School,
a near-seven-footer named Reggie Harding. For three
consecutive years Harding was selected to all-state teams,
and he went directly from high school to a contract with
the professional Detroit Pistons. Harding was four years
older than Nathaniel and lived on the other side of town,
but Nathaniel followed Reggie's career and would sometimes take a bus to the East Side to watch the big
man mess around with the kids on playground courts.
Nathaniel wasn't certain if he'd reach seven feet, but he
frequently told people that he was on the way to becoming "another Reggie Harding."

(On September 2, 1972, thirty-year-old Reginald Hez-
eriah Harding was shot twice in the head and killed
while he sat on the front porch of the home of a woman
friend in Detroit. He had played effectively for the
Detroit Pistons in his first and only season, but in 1965
he was suspended by the National Basketball Association
after being convicted of assaulting a policeman. He was
later arrested for armed robbery, carrying a concealed
weapon, and probation violations. He admitted to heroin
addiction.)

A far more significant but much less publicized black
basketball figure in Detroit in Presley's time was the
coach at Pershing High School, Will Robinson. He not
only located and nurtured potential talent but actually
passed his athletes along to colleges. Will Robinson knew
about the city game and its ramifications before most
others, black or white. He knew how to protect his
immature, unsophisticated, often scholastically un-

equipped young men from the recruiting wolves and their giddy promises. He could only tell his near-children what he thought was right. He knew most of the colleges and their coaches, and he perceived who among them was truly interested in keeping those alluring recruiting promises to his black talent. But Will also understood why most of his kids ultimately bent to the pressures. No mere high school coach could combat the temptations of big-time basketball once big-time basketball saw the wisdom of becoming a temptress.

No one was more ready to be wooed than Nathaniel Robert Presley. Events managed to get him to Pershing, and to Will Robinson, early in 1962.

Getting there was easier than staying there.

Nathaniel was ushered out of Sherrard Junior High School for truancy during his first semester and dispatched to another school in the neighborhood, the Moore School of Observation for Senior Ungraded Boys. Word was that Moore was a school for incorrigibles. But many of Moore's enrollees were either persistent truants or slow learners or both. Compatible traits: if one didn't go, one didn't learn at the recommended pace.

Moore looked like just another school building to Nathaniel, another distraction from the only thing he could stay interested in for more than ten minutes at a time: ball. At the age of fifteen, Nathaniel was single-minded. In that regard, at that time, in that city, he was not alone. Ball, and the right people to play it in the right places, was becoming a societal imperative for youngsters of the ghetto. If ever there was a good time to be tall, this was it. So it seemed.

Without a guidance counselor, without any semblance of a job in his "field," Nathaniel made a career decision:

basketball would be his life. And the goal seemed easy to him. Easy. That was the key word. Don't think about it.

He was big enough and would get bigger. He was reasonably well coordinated. He had no trouble handling himself in games with players from his age group. The game was easy, something that took little work, something that made few demands on him. As far as Nathaniel was concerned, the eventual stardom and the money it would bring was out there for him. All he had to do was wait a little while until basketball success found him. And he was certain he wouldn't be hard to find. Just a matter of time. And much easier than working.

George Gaddy, a forty-six-year-old veteran teacher and counselor, was the physical education instructor at Moore when Nathaniel was transferred. Gaddy had the ability to contend with the students, or nonstudents, assigned there. "They're socially maladjusted, if you have to pin it down with a term," said Gaddy. "Kids who never found out what they wanted to do in their lives." Another teacher classified the Moore kids as "slow thinkers."

Nathaniel was not happy. Northern. Moore. It didn't matter—he just didn't want to go to school. But he knew there could be big trouble if he failed to attend his classes. There was talk about Moore truants being punished and sent away, and he had no interest in *that* kind of trouble. So he reported to school, and an office secretary sent him immediately to the gym to see George Gaddy. The school did not have an organized athletic program, but there was a small gymnasium and sufficient games to test the abilities of the potential athletes.

Gaddy spotted him from a corner of the gym: a smiling kid coming toward him slowly, reluctantly. Gaddy picked up a basketball to test the newcomer's reactions. He threw the ball, hard, toward Nathaniel. And the big kid, continuing to walk and smile, made no effort to catch it. He just let it hit him in the face. Gaddy told him to leave the gym and wondered why he was still smiling.

Through the next several months at Moore, Gaddy tried to understand Nathaniel but reached only surface conclusions: the kid was a loner, always kept to himself; he was polite without being enthusiastic; nothing seemed to interest him except for those moments when he was alone in the gym shooting baskets. Nathaniel was not a problem to Gaddy or any of the other Moore teachers; nor was he a joy to teach. "He just doesn't seem to give a damn about school," Gaddy said. "The kid doesn't seem to care about anything." Gaddy looked for anger or stridency or pleasure or pain and always came up empty. He had to admit that he simply couldn't fathom Nathaniel Presley. At the end of the semester it was apparent to Gaddy that Nathaniel wasn't being helped, or for that matter hindered, at Moore and could probably handle a return to a regular high school. More to the point, a particular high school, one with a teacher who might best be able to plumb what Gaddy saw as Nathaniel's only interest in life: ball. Gaddy was convinced the best place for Nathaniel was Pershing High School. With Will Robinson.

Robinson, the black coach, later said that Gaddy, the black teacher, "was the guy who started the Presley ball rolling." There was no condemnation in Robinson's tone. He knew of others Gaddy tried to help and understood Gaddy's desire to save ghetto youngsters from themselves. "George thinks that it's better to save a kid for even one year than not save him at all," Robinson said. "What I always wonder is if George just didn't prolong the agony. The way it went, I was frequently George's dumping grounds. And none of the people he dumped on me ever really succeeded."

The failure might have been due as much to the nature of Pershing High as to the character of Gaddy's trans- fers. At the time Nathaniel was sent to Robinson, early in 1962, Pershing still had a sizable white enrollment. For the first time in his nearly sixteen years, Nathaniel was confronted with a new breed of people. Nothing in his life had prepared him for this.

Whites who are intimidated by the sight of a large black person seldom consider the possibility that large black persons can be unsettled by medium-sized whites. Nathaniel had grown up in a black world. In Birming- ham he saw few people beyond his father, mother, brother, and sisters. During the few months in Uncle Victor's attic in Detroit, he was more confined; even his mother was too frightened by the new environment to venture from that house. Inkster gave the Presleys a bit more space, but if Nathaniel saw one white person a day there, well, that was a crowd. And the Delmar atmos- phere was overwhelmingly black. Pershing seemed like the moon.

As he walked through the Pershing halls those first few days, he felt the stares, real or imagined, of every white student he passed. Once he pivoted quickly to catch a group of white kids who had turned around themselves and were still watching him. He had always felt self-conscious among his own; now this. His first thought in his first few minutes at Pershing was: "How the hell do I get out of Pershing?"

He told his mother, "They're all like hillbillies there.

They're all pushing me around. I know none of them can stand me 'cause I'm a big old black guy."

Edna was not sure how to respond; his predicament was new to her, too.

"Don't pay attention to them," she said. "They're supposed to be there to learn. And so are you. So go there and learn." She told Nathaniel what her grandma had told her: "Don't bother peoples, and peoples won't bother you." Edna said that this was simple, good philosophy. "I always believed it, and you should, too."

"But what if other peoples don't believe it?" Nathaniel asked.

Robert and Edna Presley knew they couldn't teach Nathaniel to cope in a white world. They'd had minimal exposure to whites themselves. As an adult, Robert had worked on a variety of assembly lines with whites. But this was work, not socializing. Edna was more gregarious, but her after-work companions were also blacks. The white world was one neither of them knew or wished to know, and it could get along perfectly well without them. Anyway, they had enough problems teaching Nathaniel how to live in a black world. The kids had to learn for themselves, just as they had. That was the way, the only realistic way, a not uncommon way among blacks and whites. The Presleys were not prepared to discuss the white world; there was no way they could have been prepared.

Nathaniel definitely wasn't ready. Not for the clothes. Or the cars. Or the blondes.

The blondes really perplexed him. He told a friend, "They all looks like movie stars. Even the fat ones. Where'd they all come from?"

"Now don't you be messin' with white stuff," the friend said. "That's bad trouble."

"Mess with 'em? Hell," Nathaniel said, "I'm too scared to even *talk* to 'em."

The blondes were unfathomable, but not the cars or clothes. Nathaniel watched many of the white kids driving to and from Pershing. Kids with what looked like their own cars. And good cars, too. "Buncha millionaires," Nathaniel told his friend.

"Maybe they's all pimps." The friend laughed.

"There ain't that many corners in that neighborhood," Nathaniel said. "They just all rich, that's all."

The clothing reinforced his belief that his white schoolmates must be folks of means. They seemed to wear something different every day. And good threads, too. If he was embarrassed about how he looked at Maybee and Sherrard and Moore, he felt humiliated now.

"That Pershing's just too fancy a place," Nathaniel said. "No place for a big old black guy like me."

Will Robinson couldn't pin down what made Nathaniel appear to be so uninterested in life. "If I could understand what his trouble is, I know I could solve it," he said. "I've done everything I can to look for it." And he did.

Immediately he put Nathaniel's Pershing life in perspective: "You don't have to learn here," Will told him. "You just have to put in an appearance. That's all you have to do here. Show up and play ball and trust me."

The coach told Edna what he'd said to Nathaniel, and she promised to cooperate to push her son to go to school. "But I don't know if we can do anything with him," she said. "It's like he doesn't have any sense. I wonder sometimes if he's crazy."

But Will didn't think Edna was serious. He believed

Nathaniel was "an easy case. He even has his own room in his house. He doesn't strike me as the typical ghetto kid. I don't see any meanness or hostility in him. Or much selfishness either," Robinson said. "He seems so docile."

By the time he reached Pershing, Nathaniel was six-seven and still growing. "Size has forced you into basketball," the coach told the kid. "But that's OK. You're a tall man in a tall man's game, and you can move better than most of the tall men." Robinson's appraisal of his young giant's basketball capacity was quite positive. "You have the size and the agility and the intelligence to play this game very well," he said. "All you have to do is apply yourself."

Robinson did not make many mistakes about many players. Three years later he cultivated Spencer Haywood. He gave the pros Ira Harge, Mel Daniels, and Ralph Simpson. Robinson knew material, and he was convinced Presley would be a player, was certain of Nathaniel's physical and mental abilities. The only question mark for Robinson was the kid's emotional state. Would Presley apply himself?

Nathaniel was happy to hear that Robinson thought he could make it in ball. He didn't disagree with the Pershing coach. He felt he could do what had to be done on the court. He learned from the playgrounds that he was all right as a player. But what was this stuff about *applying* himself? He either could play or couldn't play. And Robinson said he could play. That was enough.

Robinson worked tirelessly with Nathaniel. If the kid failed to show at Pershing in the morning, Robinson would drive over to Delmar Avenue and pick him up. Soon Will was picking him up almost every morning. They'd talk basketball for five or ten minutes; then

Nathaniel would stop talking about the sport, or switch to another subject, or simply stare out the car window and ignore the coach.

"He wasn't dumb," Will said, "but he looked to me like a person who was lost. And I couldn't get mad at him because he wasn't a mean or nasty kid. What he had was a short interest span. He just did whatever he wanted to do when he wanted to do it. And nothing else." If Nathaniel came around to the gym to tell Will he was hungry, Robinson took him to the Pershing cafeteria and bought him lunch, often Nathaniel's second lunch of the day. Robinson tried. Still, there were mornings when Will had priority duties at school and couldn't run a personal taxi service for Nathaniel Presley. On these mornings Nathaniel stayed in bed, slept late, and loafed in front of Butch Curry's store.

One afternoon, on her way home from work, Edna saw him there.

"Why aren't you over at school?" she asked.

"My pants," he said.

"What about your pants?"

"They're no good."

"Whaddya mean, no good?"

"They're only blue jeans. Only cotton. They're not good like the white kids' pants. And they're too short, too."

"Well, if pants is the only reason you're standing out here on Westminster Street, then you can stay out here till your behind wears out."

Next day, though, Edna bought Nathaniel a pair of new, stylish slacks and a pair of shoes on her way home from work. "Next time I hear you say you're not goin' to school 'cause of your clothes, you're not gonna get anything else out of me so easy," she told him. He smiled; the next day he cut all of his classes.

Within two months Nathaniel was suspended from Pershing. There was nothing Robinson could do. He couldn't make a classroom appearance for the kid.

Nathaniel and Will Robinson never met again.

For the next sixteen months, Nathaniel drifted in and out of odd jobs, in and out of Butch Curry's. He didn't do much because he didn't want to do much. He wished he were Reggie Harding or, when he thought really big, Wilt Chamberlain. On days when he wasn't working— his longest stretch of employment was five months reconditioning used cars at a garage—he'd take off for the playgrounds. He could always find a game, and he was still the best in these pickup affairs. If his team won, he stayed on the court. He kept winning and stayed all day. The smaller guys hacked at him, but he'd learned years before to live with the fouling. "Shame we can't afford to hire our own referees here on the playground," he deadpanned to his friend Bozie. "They'd put a stop to all this hackin'."

Nathaniel didn't see much of Bozie or his other old friends except from a distance, running with trouble people, bad dudes. They asked him to smoke dope with them, or come along in whatever scam they were up to, but he still avoided trouble. He knew what he didn't want.

In September 1963 he was admitted into the "special preparatory" (slow learners) classes at Northern High School. He had pushed past six-nine, an outsized tenth grader at seventeen years old.

By now he had a steady girl named Stella. She lived

in the neighborhood, also attended Northern, and was an excellent influence on Nathaniel if for no other reason than her insistence on his promptness. Every school morning she'd phone the Presley home, ask to speak to Nathaniel, and wake him with "Get up, Tree, and put on your clothes, 'cause it's time to go to school." He'd gotten used to being called Tree by this time; he still glowered when someone referred to him as "Treetop."

Stella helped him with his schoolwork, too. And there were others at Northern contributing to his basketball education.

Northern's basketball coach, Eddie Powers, was starting his forty-fourth, and final, season at the school. Powers had last taken Northern to a state championship in 1930. This year he and his assistant, Jim Trew, believed they had the material to go all the way again. The only missing ingredient was height off the bench. And so Nathaniel was permitted to enter Northern, although he was ineligible to play until the semester break early in 1964. Time enough, though, to fit with the talent at hand, kids like Bill Tally, Chuck Tolson, Al Banks, Bernie Maxwell. Nathaniel thought it kind of funny that Northern's nickname was Eskimos. "Here I am," he said laughingly to Edna one afternoon, "a giant black Eskimo. Mush!"

Assistant coach Trew worked with Presley in the few months before his eligibility. Now they were calling the kid Robert; that's how the books carried him, by his birth name, Robert Nathaniel Presley.

"Pound for pound and inch for inch, you've got as much athletic ability as anyone I've ever seen," Trew told him. Powers was also encouraging. Trew and Powers were white, as were most of the faculty at Northern, and Nathaniel had never heard this praise from whites.

Will Robinson had said nice things, but that was different to Nathaniel: one black hyping another. These words at Northern were special to him. He was encouraged and happy to play on a good team. His first real team. The excitement, and Stella's phone calls, were enough to keep him coming to school every day, not necessarily attending class every day, but at least showing up in the gym. He could spend as much time as he wanted there, shooting, shooting, shooting.

Trew and Powers were impressed by Nathaniel's shooting touch and ability to swat away shots on defense. But that's all he did on defense—stay under the hoop. He did not extend himself in practice. If his scrimmage team lost the ball after missing a shot, Nathaniel loafed returning to the other end of the court to play defense. The coaches could tell he understood this transition phase of basketball, but they couldn't get him to exert himself on the switches from offense to defense. He was too hungry for baskets.

"He's like a big, raw Saint Bernard," Trew told Powers.

When the coaches had enough of Nathaniel's loafing, one of them whistled him off the court and asked what was wrong. "Just tired," Nathaniel said. "All that defense makes me tired." And he'd be sent back to the locker room for what the coaches considered punishment. After several minutes, Tally took a break from practice himself and dragged his soon-to-be teammate back to the court. And for a while Nathaniel did hustle. And when he made an effort, when he did play all out, he genuinely thrilled Jim Trew.

"It's a pleasure," said the assistant coach, "just to see you out there, Robert. You don't know what a marvelous thing it is to watch a developing superstar."

"You mean Wilt Presley?" said the kid.

On March 20, 1964, in East Lansing, Michigan, Nathaniel played ball in front of more people than he thought existed. The crowd for the semifinal of the state's Class A high school tournament was over twelve thousand. Two hours before tipoff time Nathaniel took a seat in the top row of the arena to get a fan's perspective. "From up here," he told Tally, "I'll be a little black ant."

Presley's play with the Eskimos had been erratic leading up to the state tournament. Powers used him as a reserve center, bringing him in when he wanted to rest Tolson or when he needed rebounding help. Powers was patient with the big kid because this was Nathaniel's first real competitive experience. But the coach showed his anger when Nathaniel ignored team play and dribbled the ball down the foul lane or on the baseline behind the basket instead of passing off to a teammate. Nathaniel had spent too many years on the playground to shed his love for one-on-one basketball.

"Stop putting the ball on the floor so much," Powers grunted during a time-out.

"But I can beat my man, coach," Nathaniel said. "I knows I can beat him."

"I don't care if you can beat him. There are four other guys wearing the same kinda uniform you are."

Northern defeated Saginaw 75–56 in the semifinal game of the state tourney. The Eskimos led by only three points, 30–27, at the half, but then put the game away in the opening moments of the third period with fine shooting by Tally, Tolson, and Presley. In a brief appearance during that spurt, Nathaniel hit four buckets.

"What a shooting touch," said Northern teacher Bill

Lajoie. "So soft. The net would just slightly ruffle when his shot went in."

"Presley quickly caught the fancy of the huge crowd," wrote the man from the *Detroit Free Press.*

Next morning Nathaniel read about himself and told Tally, "Look at me, a fancy Tree."

In the final game, played twenty-four hours after the semifinal round, Northern played Benton Harbor, which had a habit of beating favored, bigger teams. But in this game Benton Harbor was favored; few of the experts believed the inner-city kids could stand the pressure of the tournament.

At the half, Northern had built a 37–27 bulge. The Eskimos contained Benton Harbor's all-state forward, L. C. Bowen, and continued to clamp him through the third period. Bowen had scored only ten points in the first twenty-four minutes, and Northern led 52–46. Bowen was a good clutch shooter, particularly down the stretch, but so far this night Tally was the big scorer.

Nathaniel was on the floor at the start of the final quarter. Powers sent him into the game in the last minute of the third period when Tolson fouled out. Because he'd played so well the night before, the crowd gave him a warm reception. Tolson had scored only eight points, and Northern fans figured that his departure on fouls wouldn't be crucial, not the way Presley had played Friday.

"Play good defense," Powers told Nathaniel. "Help out guarding Bowen. What I want you to do when Bowen has the ball is come out to the free throw line, hold up your arms, and intimidate the hell out of him. Don't let him drive the lane."

Nathaniel was too nervous to answer.

In his first minute of play, he fouled Bowen. In the

first three minutes of the final quarter, he picked up four more fouls, three while trying to guard Bowen, one for charging while attempting to drive on Bowen.

Bowen's free throws chipped away at the Northern lead, but more devastating was the fact that Presley had fouled out with more than five minutes remaining in the game. Powers had no height left on his bench, no one to stop Bowen.

The Benton Harbor star began hitting baskets, brought his team to a tie at 65 with 3:15 to play, put his team ahead to stay at 2:55. Bowen scored fifteen points in the last quarter; Benton Harbor won, 78–73.

Nathaniel had tried to play one-on-one basketball with L. C. Bowen and emerged from the experience with one basket and five fouls.

The *Free Press* account of the championship game identified Nathaniel as "Tom Pressley."

The end of the season was tantamount to the end of Nathaniel's record of consistent attendance at Northern. He knew—had been told—that he would be the Eskimos' first-string center the next season. But that was far away, beyond an empty summer and tedious fall. "I just can't get up for the rest of school," he told Tally, and began cutting classes again on a regular basis.

Stella wasn't making her morning phone calls either. Soon after the state tournament she'd found another boyfriend. Edna Presley could tell her son was hurt.

Early in May, Nathaniel joined a group loitering in front of a doughnut shop across the street from Northern. The guys were sipping out of wine bottles concealed in brown bags. He stayed with them for nearly two hours, then giddily announced, "I think it's time to take the Tree to the school." He walked, drunk, into Northern High.

An English teacher, Bob Steen, noticed the large, weaving young man. He said something Nathaniel could not decipher. But Nathaniel did not like what he could not hear; Steen, he assumed, was being critical. So he jumped him.

Five other teachers, including Trew and Lajoie, were summoned to help pull Presley off the English teacher. For several minutes Trew and Nathaniel rolled on the floor in the school corridor. The brawling continued for more than ten minutes as Nathaniel kept thrashing and shoving teachers. Finally, Trew, with plenty of help, was able to drag Presley into a nearby study hall.

"He's so drunk he can barely stand," Trew said. Nathaniel heard him and leaped at the assistant coach. Again the teachers subdued the big kid. Trew took off his own belt and tied it around Nathaniel's feet, and the police came. While officers were putting Nathaniel into their car, he kicked one of them in the head.

Nathaniel was booked, jailed, bailed to his father that evening. The next day he was suspended indefinitely from Northern High School. His name made the papers for the third time: "CAGE STAR RUNS AMOK" headlined the *Detroit News*. And Presley's friend Bill Tally, the team captain, also was suspended for being on the fringe of the wine-soaked melee.

A week later Edna took her son to the office of Northern principal Arthur Carty. "They'll never let me back in," Nathaniel said to his mother. "I'm finished at Northern."

They spent nearly an hour with the principal. Edna told Nathaniel to apologize for being "overruled by wine." And he did. Edna said they would pray. She talked and pleaded and tried to charm Carty. But the suspension held.

When they walked out of the principal's office, Edna had the impression that Nathaniel was sweating. But she looked more closely and saw tears.

"I hate to see you cry," she said. "You're too big to cry like that."

She began to weep herself. He had brought this trouble on himself, she thought, but she had failed because she couldn't convince the principal to let Nathaniel back into school.

As they walked toward home, Nathaniel lingered a few paces behind his mother. "This isn't the end of the world," she said. "Just because you failed in there doesn't mean you're all finished. You stop making mistakes, and there'll be another day for you."

A student walking on the other side of the street called out, "Hey, Tree, how you make out with the man?"

"I didn't," Nathaniel shouted back.

He crossed the street to talk with the other kid, and Edna walked the rest of the way alone.

And at his desk in the school, Principal Carty made a notation on Nathaniel's record to pass along to whatever—if any—school next accepted the young man. "Robert Presley," wrote Carty, "has an inability to adjust in any comprehensive school situation."

George Gaddy was unhappy with the disposition of Nathaniel's case at Northern. "They shouldn't have called the police," he said. "They should have sobered him up and then let him walk out of the building by himself." Now the best thing for Nathaniel, Gaddy decided, was to get out of Detroit. Trouble like this only brought worse trouble. At least Nathaniel had been put on probation. "I've got to get him out of town before he's killed," Gaddy said. He would have to make connections, write a few letters out West where he knew people interested in big kids who could play ball.

Gaddy had established plenty of contacts in California. He had found places for athletes and nonathletes. But it was always easier if the kid to be placed was tall and athletic.

By late October 1964, Gaddy had arranged a transfer for Nathaniel, but the kid showed no interest. One late afternoon in mid-November, Gaddy was driving along Woodward and saw Nathaniel standing at a bus stop. The temperature was near zero. Gaddy pulled over to the curb and rolled down a window. "You're crazy to be outside in this cold when you could be in California. If you want to go to California, you call me."

Nathaniel didn't respond. Gaddy rolled up the window and drove off.

The next day Gaddy got a call from Nathaniel. California would be real fine with him, said the young man. Could Gaddy talk to his parents for a minute? How soon could he leave for California? He was ready right now.

Edna Presley was now on the phone. "Will Nathaniel be all right?" she said.

Gaddy assured her there was nothing to worry about. "He'll be a lot better off out there." And Edna said that would be just fine with the Presley family. No arguments. No need for elaboration.

A month later Nathaniel was on a Greyhound bus en route to Salinas, California. He had boarded a 1964 version of the Underground Railroad.

5

THE BUS TRIP took sixty hours, including a transfer in San Francisco. Nathaniel had a double seat to himself most of the way. His father had given him a few dollars to tide him over until he found a part-time job in Salinas, and Edna made him a bagful of ham sandwiches. He nursed the food for two and one-half days and bought Cokes, candy bars, and pieces of pie at the rest stops.

He didn't know anything about Salinas, but he didn't care. Gaddy told him he'd have a good chance to play ball in California, first for Salinas High School and then for a junior college. Gaddy didn't specify what junior college; he told Nathaniel to behave himself and everything would work out.

Nathaniel didn't know how these things worked. Here he was, a suspended tenth grader from Detroit about to start the eleventh grade at a new high school in another state. This confused him, but he knew he was getting away from a place where not much good had happened to him. And that was fine. Salinas might be OK; it couldn't be worse.

He remembered hearing Gaddy say, "Coaches from all over the country write to ask me to recommend kids. These coaches get their brains beat out by some team and they ask the coach who beat 'em, 'Where'd that great colored kid come from?' And one coach tells the other to write to me. I've got my kids spread all over—Texas, West Virginia, California, everywhere."

An hour out of Chicago Nathaniel paced the bus aisle to keep from atrophying. The second time he passed two young black men seated together. One of them waved at him to sit in the empty seat across the way. They introduced themselves as Raymond and Stanley. Raymond was light-skinned and had a wisp of a goatee. Stanley was as black as Nathaniel and from his crumpled position in the bus seat looked about as tall. They said they were on their way home to Richmond, California, near San Francisco, for Thanksgiving vacation. They both went to a small college in Wisconsin. They both played ball and asked where he played ball.

For the next two hours, Raymond and Stanley talked to Nathaniel about basketball gypsies. They told him that he was doing what they had done, except in a reverse geographical direction.

He told them about George Gaddy. "We've got our own Gaddy back home," said Stanley. "There's one of him in every ghetto. College recruiters come to town lookin' for a big black guy who can play. They always check in first with a man like Gaddy 'cause he knows who's available and who's wantin' to leave town."

"The recruiters look you over," said Raymond, "and if you can play, they just sign you right up. As long as you got your high school diploma, you can get into somebody's college. If you can play."

Nathaniel complained that he'd have to wait two years, until he finished high school, to play for a college. "Here I am eighteen," he said. "Seems like I've been goin' to one high school or another forever."

"No problem," said Raymond. "In California you can go to high school and college at the same time. That's why you be comin' out to California."

This made no sense to Nathaniel.

"In California," Raymond continued, "it's perfectly legal to start goin' to a junior college even before you graduate high school. All you got to do is live in the junior college district. And just about any place you live in California there's a junior college district. Hey, there's more junior colleges in California than trees."

"They're all workin' together to get good players," said Stanley.

"Hell," said Raymond, "some of those jaycee coaches are so hard up, they'll even take the leftovers. Or they'll go a couple thousand miles outa the district to Deeeee-troit, Michigan." Raymond and Stanley laughed, and Nathaniel smiled so as not to seem dense.

"I remember a few months ago there was this white guy watchin' us play," said Nathaniel. "Me and Tally and some other guys. This white guy just stood out there under the hoop on one end and looked at us. Didn't say nothin' to nobody. And somebody told me he was a junior college coach from someplace. Maybe it was California."

"Lookin' for meat," said Raymond.

Nathaniel pushed back his seat and sat quietly digesting this information. He found it funny and interesting. He wasn't sure what it all had to do with him.

Nathaniel arrived in Salinas early on the morning of

November 23, 1964, put his bag in a locker at the bus station, and walked to Salinas High School. A secretary in the principal's office told him to report to the gymnasium to basketball coach Russ Messner. The coach told him to wait and went to confer with school counselor and psychology teacher Gordon Ray. In a few minutes Nathaniel was summoned to Ray's office. Within the hour, as Bob Presley, Nathaniel was enrolled in the eleventh grade of Salinas High.

He had made it through the Underground Railroad. For the moment.

Ray was fascinated by the informality of Bob Presley's arrival in his counseling office.

"I'm sending this kid up to see you," Coach Messner told him. "He's had some problems back East, but now he's moved here. Help him in any way you can to get enrolled in classes."

Ray was thirty-three and a sports buff. One of his diversions was manning the public address system at the football games at Hartnell Junior College. He knew all the coaches and many of the athletes at both Salinas High and Hartnell, which was only a half-dozen blocks away from the high school. He was sympathetic to the scholastic problems of athletes.

But the nature of Presley's arrival surprised him; no student had ever been thrust upon him like this. He never questioned Messner, though. If there were anything else he was supposed to know about this kid, Russ would tell him.

"I'll help you in any way I can," Ray said to Bob at their first meeting, "but it'll be tough to get you into the right classes. Most of the teachers here don't give athletes any special treatment. But if you work with me and concentrate, I'll help you get through." Bob was relieved: a white man in a strange town was willing to help him.

Ray enrolled Bob in six courses, including his own psychology class. Even though he was entering Salinas High more than two months after the semester started, Bob passed all but one of the courses. "He did most of the back work, and the teachers and students warmed up to him right away," said Ray. Bob *was* trying. He studied because there was not much else to do in town. He particularly enjoyed reading one section of the psychology textbook, the part on "understanding yourself." His main understanding was that if he made grades and kept out of trouble, he could soon be eligible to play ball someplace; then everything would fall into line for him.

Bob lived briefly with several other out-of-state black athletes in a row of small shacks once used by migrant farm workers. The housing, and jobs, were financed by a group of Hartnell sports fans who wished to make sure the jaycee's athletes didn't have serious financial problems. In a letter to Edna, Bob called the housing "like living in a chicken coop." He complained to his mother that he wasn't getting enough to eat. But he wrote that he'd stick it out as long as he could; pretty soon he was going to be a star player for somebody.

But Bob was not eligible to play basketball until he could become a resident of the school district. That was not in Ray's domain—somebody else would have to deal with it. Salinas High coach Messner wasn't about to tamper with any records; Messner was an unbending follower of rules. Not all coaches were.

A junior college sports import often becomes an automatic "resident" of a school district, even though his parents live a few thousand miles away. In some cases, the player suddenly has a local guardian; in the extreme, if a guardianship can't be arranged, records show that the player lives with his parents in the new district. And in the ultimate extreme, if officials of the athletic conference are bent on spot-checking these residency arrangements, parents are flown to the new home of their son, to be on hand if somebody comes around to inspect.

If anyone was going to take care of Bob Presley's residency problems, Ray was convinced it would be Hartnell basketball coach Bill Martinson. Martinson, not yet thirty-five, was an ambitious, intense coach, starting his first full season at Hartnell. He stayed just that one year. Martinson had been a track star at Baylor; he believed he could deal with black athletes because he'd run with them in college. Before taking the Hartnell job he coached basketball in high schools in the Northwest and Alaska. Bill Martinson was the coach who'd seen Presley and Tally playing in Detroit earlier in 1964. He'd been looking for players—for himself and for a few coaching friends at four-year colleges. Martinson considered himself an excellent recruiter. He talked to Gaddy and arranged for Tally to come to the Salinas area, to Gonzales High School first and then to Hartnell. But Presley's old Northern teammate couldn't adjust to California and went back to Detroit within the year.

Martinson admitted setting up this arrangement for Tally. But he denied being Bob Presley's sponsor on the Underground Railroad, although Ray and others in Salinas insisted that Martinson was Presley's logistical coordinator.

Gaddy said he didn't remember his link in Salinas. "There were so many people I knew, and it was so long ago," said Gaddy.

"Gaddy called me," said Martinson, "and asked me if I could use Presley. I told him, 'Who the hell can't use a guy seven foot tall?' I didn't know who the hell was involved in getting him out to Salinas. I didn't even ask. Then I get a phone call one day, and here he was in Salinas. Right out of the blue. I talked to Coach Messner at the high school because I was as interested in Bob doing well for him as for us later on. And Messner wanted him to play. I thought Bob was going to play there."

An attempt was made in Salinas to provide a guardian for Bob Presley. Martinson said a black police officer wanted to become Bob's guardian. The officer talked to Ray about guardianship plans, and Edna then received a phone call seeking her approval for a guardianship arrangement, but she was never sent any papers to sign. And the policeman left Salinas in late 1965; he has not been heard of since. He never became Bob's guardian.

In February 1965, Bob enrolled for the second semester at Salinas. He still didn't have enough credits to be eligible to play ball in the high school's few remaining games that season. He was frustrated, tired of waiting.

A few weeks after the semester began, he told Martinson, "I'm eighteen years old and I can go to your college and frankly I don't want to play that high school ball." Martinson didn't blame him, "because that was Mickey Mouse compared to what he could play."

"You gotta do what you gotta do," said the counselor.

So Bob dropped out of Salinas High on February 16 and signed up for a few classes at Hartnell.

"Don't bother anybody," Martinson told him. "Don't

pat any white girls on the fanny." Martinson always believed that Northern ghetto blacks were more trouble than their Southern counterparts. "The Southern blacks were good kids," he said. "They tried. The Northern blacks were different. They even controlled the blacks from the South if they were on the same team together." But Bob didn't try to control anybody at Hartnell. He wasn't there that long. He didn't want to wait for the next basketball season to begin in October.

He had made a few bucks teaching basketball in a neighborhood recreation center and had enough money to buy a bus ticket back to Detroit in late April. He wrote Edna and told her he was coming home, that the people in Salinas wouldn't let him play ball, that he didn't want to stick around there if he couldn't play.

She accepted his judgment and told Robert to ask the people at Ford if they'd give Nathaniel some work in the plant's maintenance department. By the time Bob came home, a job was waiting.

He was now nineteen years old, a half inch under seven feet tall, and still not finished with the eleventh grade. He didn't care if he ever went back to school again. He had worked hard in those classes at Salinas High. What did all that work get him? He was too old for high school now anyway. The little kids in high school would laugh at him if he went back now. He couldn't bear that. And as Detroit turned on its summertime blast furnace, Bob wondered if he could bear Detroit anymore. The weather in California had spoiled him. It was much more relaxed, too; a man could go at his own pace there. He wanted to ask Gaddy if he could line up another college out there for him. But Bob hated to ask anyone for help, even Gaddy.

He was seeing Gaddy regularly because in his off-hours from Ford he was playing on the team at George's recreation center. The team was called the "Collegians": Some of them actually were. Bob enjoyed the competition but was annoyed that the results of the games and his performances were ignored outside the ghetto.

But Gaddy didn't ignore Bob's ball abilities. In late summer he made arrangements for Bob with another contact—this one in Southern California. A friend of a friend needed all the players he could get at his junior college. And this friend of this friend promised to be patient with Bob, help him finish his high school work, make it through the jaycee, and play all the ball he wanted.

Bob tried to hide his enthusiasm when Gaddy told him about the arrangements. But by the time he got home to tell Edna, he wasn't sure this new trip was worth getting excited about.

"Just more school," he told his mother. "High school classes. Junior college classes. I'll be goin' to school twenty-five hours a day. I'll be too tired to play ball. I'll have to do my homework between free throws and during time-outs. It'll be a lot easier stayin' here."

Edna would be happy to have Bob at home that year. She was disappointed that the Salinas experience hadn't worked out for him, yet she did worry about him when he was away. He seemed to need so much. Not that she and Robert could provide much for him, but here in Detroit he could learn to manage just as they had. Still, maybe it would be wrong for him to pass up this new opportunity.

"Not everybody gets a second chance like this," said Edna, "and maybe it'll be better for you out there this time."

"I guess there's nothin' to lose," said Bob. And he bought another bus ticket West.

Mount San Jacinto Junior College didn't look like much of a college to Bob. It didn't look like much of anything except a warehouse, which is what it was: an old lumber warehouse converted into a classroom building, an infant institution of semihigher learning created to serve two hundred young adults in the nearby desert towns of Hemet and Banning. Plush Palm Springs was about a half hour west, but Hemet and Banning were just a couple of dots people drove through en route to Arizona.

Bob made the long bus trip with another player from Detroit, John Q. Trapp. They'd known each other back home only vaguely, from games on playgrounds and in rec centers. Trapp had played a little ball with Reggie Harding, and during the ride West he talked about Reggie, who had just finished his first successful season in the pros. "Are you gonna be a superstar?" a writer asked Harding that year. And Reggie replied, "Is the sun gonna shine?"

Trapp told Bob that Harding always carried a basketball around with him. "Even slept with the damn thing," said Trapp. Bob told Trapp he wanted more than anything to be like Reggie Harding.

Dan Ayala was Mount San Jacinto's basketball coach, fresh from coaching high school ball in Banning. He was a Chicano who played and taught ball in a white world. He knew it would take some time to build a fairly good team in this boondock: it was impossible to recruit talent overnight. Ayala was patient with himself and his athletes. He could not expect too much too quickly.

Ayala found a room for Trapp and Presley in the home of an elderly black couple, the Browns. He arranged for Bob to finish his high school requirements in Banning and at the same time pick up credits at the jaycee. Until Bob received his high school diploma, he couldn't play for Mount San Jacinto. So Ayala preached patience, a sermon Bob had heard so many times before.

Bob worked out with the team regularly in the 1965–66 season, adjusting to the jaycee level of basketball. Trapp and Presley had no social life. They kept to their room and, even while in the room, to themselves. Ayala had them busy working and studying. The routine soon got to Trapp, and within a few months he transferred to another California junior college. But Bob hung on.

Ayala had him in a work-study program that provided seventy-five dollars a month. The work was as a campus maintenance man and every day Bob attacked weeds with a hoe. He couldn't loaf because his assigned area was just outside the window of the school's president, Milo Johnson, who often watched Ayala's giant. "He's a pretty diligent young man," the president told the coach.

Diligent, and poor. Bob picked up a few extra bucks baby-sitting with Ayala's three children, but he lacked money for clothes and transportation. "Just wait," Ayala told him. "It'll come."

Toward the end of the first semester, Bob moved out of the Browns' home and into an apartment. Mr. Brown kept bugging him to go to church. "If I went every time he told me to," said Bob, "I wouldn't be able to study or work." He did maintenance chores at his new apartment building and paid rent of only twenty-five dollars a month. And he saved on food expenses by eating with the basketball team, whose training table was a smorgasbord restaurant in Hemet.

With the three jobs—weeding, baby-sitting, working around the apartment building—and with the break in food costs, Bob met his essential expenses of about ninety dollars a month.

"There's so much I want to do," he told Ayala, "but there's never enough money to do anything."

"What would you do if you did have a few bucks?" asked the coach.

"First thing, I'd send some home to my mother. I want to help her, but I know I can't, at least not for a while. I don't know if I ever can help her."

"Don't worry," said Ayala. "Just do the best you can, and something might happen."

The coach respected Presley. He wondered occasionally about Bob's vacant look of depression, but he ascribed those down moments to the loneliness of a nineteen-year-old far from home and to worries about what tomorrow might bring, if anything.

"You've got a big future," Ayala often told him.

"The only future I got time to concentrate on is what's for supper," said Bob.

There was so much to do that Bob didn't have time to be too depressed. His alternative back home was sweeping floors at Ford. Here, at least, something might happen. He didn't mind jumping around from Banning High to the jaycee to work to Ayala's house to the apartment building to practice to studying. He was meeting a challenge. He'd never done that. He was never sure he could. It was as if he was proving something to himself.

Trapp didn't make it there, but he did. That was *one* for him.

Ayala told his friends and other coaches that Presley was an obvious pro prospect. In Dan's view, Bob would make a fine big college center and then ascend to the pros. He was coachable, amenable to learning, able to execute the fundamentals. Bob's only real problem at this stage was to keep from tripping over his own feet on picks and patterns and fast breaks, but that was remedial. Most big kids lack pedal coordination in the early stages of their basketball development. Ayala was certain Bob could become a graceful player. He'd make the adjustment to the game all right, but the coach wondered if Bob could deal with the community—with the whites.

At the team meals at the smorgasbord in Hemet, Bob sailed into the all-you-can-eat buffet spread as if he could eat it all twice. His weight in those two years at Mount San Jacinto went from a gawky 185 pounds to 240. "I owe my strength to the smorgasbord potato salad," he said. But he was never at ease there.

"He could see the other customers staring at him," said Ayala. "We all could see them staring."

"If I was white, they wouldn't notice me," Bob said. "But I'm black and six-eleven, and they all pay attention."

"Listen," said Ayala, "there's nothing you and I can do to change human nature."

Bob scowled at this. "Maybe I'll just have to change *my* nature." Sometimes he had another player, a white player, refill his plate at the smorgasbord table. He didn't want to risk losing his temper with one of the staring white patrons.

Bob stayed in California in the summer of 1966. He didn't want to waste the little money he had on a bus ticket home. And he was beginning to enjoy the atmosphere at Mount San Jacinto. He knew he'd be playing ball for the jaycee in a few months. He could hear people touting his impending stardom. He liked being a big fish in this small desert pond. He *was* becoming a somebody.

The coach got Bob a handyman's job paying $1.40 an hour and settled his budding center in a less expensive apartment in nearby Gilman Hot Springs, a boxers' training camp. Bob was able to save a few dollars for clothes. He zipped through his few remaining courses at Banning High; he was finally, at the age of twenty, a high school graduate. And eligible for competitive basketball. He couldn't have been more confident.

The season reflected that confidence. Bob averaged twenty-one points and eighteen rebounds a game. He was named to the all-California junior college team. Mount San Jacinto had a record of twenty-five wins and only five losses in the 1966–67 season. Major college coaches were coming down to the desert for a look.

"There are ten universities I can go to for an interview," Bob wrote Edna. "I don't know which one to see."

Ayala told sportswriters that Bob was fast for a big man, but he needed more competition to be pushed to his full potential. "He's playing against smaller men so often, he relaxes too much."

Recruiters knew about Bob's spotty juvenile record in Detroit. When they talked to Ayala, they asked the jaycee coach what kind of person Presley was *now*. Academically, he was fine, at a C-plus level. "He applies himself in class," Ayala told the flesh hunters from the

University of Southern California, Arizona, Arizona
State, Utah, Utah State, and the University of California
at Berkeley.

Bob had a problem with only one class in his two years
at San Jacinto, and that involved a personality conflict
with the instructor rather than the subject matter itself.
Bob told Ayala he was being unfairly graded in this class.
Ayala checked, found that Bob was telling the truth, and
then asked the teacher to lay off.

"Bob's a jewel," Ayala told the university recruiters
and coaches. "He's coachable. He goes to classes. He's
straight. You be straight with him, and he'll do the job
for you."

What particularly pleased Ayala was the fact that Bob
came to every practice, and the workouts began at six in
the morning at the Hemet High School gym. The jaycee
didn't have a gym of its own, and Ayala had to take what
he could get when he could get it. What he got was
Hemet High from six to eight every morning. He picked
up Bob daily and drove him to Hemet. Maybe he'd
spoken with Will Robinson.

Bob was confused by the salesmanship of the big
school recruiters. Most of the schools sounded just fine to
him; most of the fringes they offered were OK. One day
he favored one school, the next day another. He was so
eager for the next step, he was ready to succumb to
whichever recruiter he'd last seen.

"I could go on with this thing forever," he said to
Ayala in spring 1967. "If some school I never heard of
came here looking for me tomorrow, I'd probably like
them, too. I just don't know what to do."

But then he'd shift; he'd consider going back to Detroit. Too much confusion. "Anyway," he said, "I can't

make it through a big college. I'm not good enough to make the grades. I'd only flunk out, and then I couldn't play ball. Where'd I be then?"

"They'll give you special tutoring," Ayala said. "And don't forget: you made your grades here; you can make 'em again. Don't be getting down on yourself. You're only a few months away. All the good things are out there waiting for you. Don't forget that. After you play at a big university, the future will be unlimited for you. Keep that in mind."

Ayala didn't want Bob to go to just any large school. The coach believed that what Bob needed was an *understanding* large school; specifically, a school with a coach who would care about Bob as a person as much as a player. "A college coach will have to realize that Bob is a little sensitive," Ayala told a colleague. "Bob's just starting to feel his way around. There's no question about what he can do in the game, but whatever college ends up with him is going to have to take their time with him. They're going to have to treat him delicately. If they do that, it'll be worth it to them."

Presley had to be *handled*. That's what Ayala was talking about: handling.

There are three facets of coaching basketball at a major college today: recruiting, handling, coaching. A coach who is ineffective at the first two duties has trouble getting a job—no matter how able a tactician he may be. If he lacks the personality to recruit good players, he won't have a team to put on the court, whatever his level of coaching genius. If he is amiable enough to land talent, he must know how to keep this talent content, soothed. If he doesn't, if he is unable to handle these players with a blend of patience, caring, and skillful discipline, he ends up with an emotional hodgepodge on the floor—whatever his level of coaching genius.

A coach who has the five best players does not necessarily have the best basketball team. But the coach who knows how to recruit, handle, and then coach will almost always win.

At the time Bob Presley was playing for Mount San Jacinto, one of the best recruiters in California was a white named Jim Padgett. He had a fine record of recruiting and handling black players while coaching at San Jose City College, and he had just become an assistant coach at the University of California at Berkeley. Dan Ayala figured Padgett was the discerning kind of handler Presley needed. Also, Ayala had great respect for the head coach at Berkeley, Rene Herrerias, a Chicano like Ayala. Dan believed Berkeley was just the right spot for Bob; he'd be handled by Padgett and coached by the tactically sound Herrerias.

"You should go to Berkeley," Ayala told Bob.

"But it's so big," said Presley. "What I keep hearing is that you can get swallowed up in Berkeley."

"Padgett won't let that happen to you," said Ayala. "He helps the players with schoolwork. And I'm sure he's going to help you. He'll get you as much help as you need to make grades."

Bob met Padgett several times in Banning. He found the recruiter loose and easy to talk to. "The man cares," said Bob. "The man's OK. I dig him."

After the last session with Padgett, Bob came to Ayala's office. "Tell all those other schools to cool it," he said. "I'm goin' to Berkeley."

When Bob moved from Banning to Berkeley in the summer of 1967, it was as if he'd been transported from an oasis into a volcano.

On the one hand, Cal was cited by the American Council on Education as the nation's "best balanced distinguished university." On the other, California's state superintendent of schools had a few months earlier called the university "a sanctuary for odd birds." The new governor, Ronald Reagan, after promising in his campaign to "clean up the mess" on campus, had cut the school's budget by 29 percent.

The Black Panther party, based on the Berkeley-Oakland border, was making its way into national headlines. Across the Bay in San Francisco that summer there was a combined upsurge of flower children and war protestors. A minority student program, pressured into existence by militants, had just started on the Cal campus, and a militant Stokely Carmichael turned up to lead a Black Power Conference.

His first day on campus, Bob met a football player in the athletic department offices who told him, "There's something really big going on here every day. You can't keep track. Every day, something else."

But the basketball program at Cal had been the essence of stability. There had been only three basketball coaches at Berkeley in forty-three years. Nibs Price ran the show from 1924 to 1954, when he was succeeded by Pete Newell.

Twice in six seasons Newell led Cal to the finals of the National Collegiate Athletic Association tournament, winning the title in 1959 and finishing second the following year. Newell was succeeded as head coach in the 1960–61 season by Rene Herrerias, his former player at the University of San Francisco and longtime assistant coach. Newell stepped up to the athletic directorship.

Herrerias was Newell's boy, an able coach, a near-carbon of his mentor. He was considered a master tactician and, in fact, had a greater textbook knowledge of the game than Newell. When he was Newell's assistant, Herrerias was the team's chief scout, and his reports on upcoming opponents were considered masterpieces by the players. Pete and Rene quizzed the players in the locker room before a game, and everybody on the team, even the last sub, had to participate. "By the time you got on the court," said one of their players, "you knew every single thing about every single strength and weakness on the opposition. You were totally ready, completely psyched up."

Newell's players considered Herrerias a co-coach. At halftime it was Herrerias who diagrammed plays and defenses on the locker room blackboard while Newell spoke. And Herrerias attended to all of the small, off-court player problems. He was not as glib or worldly as Newell, but he was efficient and always available. To the players, Newell was the steel, Rene the warmth.

"Whenever I raised hell with the players, Rene kept the lid on," said Newell. "As an assistant, he related masterfully to the kids."

The coaches told the players to call them Pete and Rene, but when a player needed a shoulder to cry on about grades or extra tickets or minor perquisites, the athletes looked to Herrerias. He may have lacked Newell's outgoing nature, but he was the player's friend, the perfect assistant, the big brother figure in the "family" atmosphere Newell instilled on his Cal teams. Teams that were almost totally white.

Racism had nothing to do with the composition of Newell's teams. Herrerias, after all, was himself a Mexican who grew up in San Francisco's rough Mission District. His basketball ability and desire to learn propelled the small guard to USF and, under Newell, a National Invitational Tournament title in 1949. After college he coached at his high school alma mater, St. Ignatius, in San Francisco. When Newell came to Cal from Michigan State, he summoned Rene across the Bay.

Together they recruited the one type of player they most valued, a player much like themselves: an intelligent, poised, *thinking* athlete.

By the time Rene inherited the head coaching job, there simply weren't enough of these players to go around. Basketball was becoming the city game, a black game. John Wooden was luring quality black players to UCLA, another school in California's conference. And Wooden was winning. Rene, however, was slow to adjust to this new recruiting posture. In his first seven seasons as head coach, his team finished as high as third in the conference only once. His job was not endangered as long as Newell ran the athletic department. But Herrerias needed to recruit for the future. And he was having trouble. He didn't know the territory.

Ned Averbuck was recruited in the 1950s by Newell and Herrerias out of East Los Angeles and later became an assistant to Herrerias. "When they talked to me, they said they'd teach me basketball and that I would learn to love, enjoy, and appreciate the game." Minimal scholarship offers. No deals. Nothing under the table. That was Newell's recruiting style, and Herrerias followed suit.

"Rene may have been too idealistic," said Dave Maggard, an Olympic shotputter and later track coach and athletic director at Berkeley. "He expected the athletes he recruited to show maturity, to go to class, to respect his ideals, to grow to adulthood. And so as head coach he had difficulty dealing with what was going on at colleges at that time—meaning the giving of your energy and time and emotion to your athletes. Not just putting X's and O's on a blackboard. He didn't want to do things that he didn't think were in the head coach's realm. He didn't want to have to hold an athlete's hand. His ideals were just too high."

The new players, the black players, were being dazzled by the verbal footwork of other big school head-hunters. They were being sold. Herrerias was neither dazzler nor salesman.

Furthermore, when a black player was lured to visit the Berkeley campus, he immediately sensed the stodginess of the athletic department and the starchiness of the "Old Blues," Cal's sports-loving alumni. Berkeley didn't look good to a black athlete then; Cal simply didn't know how to go about recruiting black players.

Herrerias's chief recruiter was a former Cal player named Bob Blake. Blond, blue-eyed, and, in the estimation of Averbuck, "the kind of guy blacks just couldn't relate to." Newell appraised Blake as "a lot like Rene, a real nice person and a good basketball mind. He taught well. But he was not a salesman." And so Blake left in 1965.

"Rene and I talked in broad terms about what kind of assistant coach we needed for our basketball program," said Newell. "Recruiting was accelerating all up and down the coast. We had to step things up ourselves. And Rene acknowledged he couldn't do this part of the job."

Newell and Herrerias received a recommendation from a friend, San Jose State coach Stu Inman. The recommendation was for the coach at San Jose City College, Jim Padgett. Pete and Rene checked him out. "He had a superior reputation as a recruiter," said Newell. Padgett was hired. He was thirty-three years old, some six years Herrerias's junior. He was a salesman, a white who could sell blacks.

"I just recruited the best players I could," he said. "I had no pipeline to the ghetto. Nothing like that. My reputation was just established through the players I was able to get, and your best recruiters are your players."

In one of his successful San Jose City seasons, Padgett had ten black players on a twelve-man roster. His six-year record at the junior college was 134 and 49.

"I've got a great recruiter coming," Herrerias told Averbuck. "I don't know if Jim is a great coach, but recruiting is what's important right now. I can always teach him to be a good coach. I don't want to know what he's doing while he's out there recruiting. All I know is, I need help. We've got to keep up with the competition, and I think Padgett can do that for us."

He did it quickly.

Bob Presley's teammates at Cal in the 1967–68 season included three black sophomores: prep high-jump record holder Clarence Johnson from San Antonio, Texas; high school all-American Trent Gaines from Long Beach, California; and game-smart Waddell Blackwell from Homestead, Pennsylvania.

Waiting in the wings, on that year's freshman team, were two other first-rate black prospects: Charles Johnson from across the Bay in Redwood City, and Jackie Ridgle, Padgett's prize, a crown jewel in recruiting. People in Arkansas said Jackie Ridgle was the greatest high school player in the entire history of the state.

The 1967–68 season was to be a break-in year, the following season promised grandeur. Herrerias would have six black stars to coach in 1968–69.

6

―――

BERKELEY WAS NOT as bountiful as Bob had expected. Down at Mount San Jacinto, Padgett had never discussed specifics, but from the enthusiastic tone and the upbeat glow exuded by the assistant Cal coach, Bob assumed that life would be beautiful once he made the move: instant fame, an easy glide through classwork, sufficient pocket money, wheels whenever he wanted them, comfortable living quarters, and any other perquisites due a campus superstar. "Somebody led Bob Presley to expect something that perhaps really wasn't there," said Dave Maggard.

What was there in Berkeley in the summer of 1967 was alternately tantalizing and depressing for Bob. His publicity was favorable. And Padgett seemed to be a good friend, always around when Bob wanted to talk, always willing to answer questions, kibitz, play a little cards, joke, discuss ball. Anything.

Bob needed a scholastic major and selected journalism with the distant notion that maybe he could be a sportswriter. Padgett introduced him to a journalism professor over a cup of coffee at the Union cafeteria patio, and the curriculum was arranged. Nothing to that; a greasing of the scholastic skids.

If Presley hadn't been an athlete, the odds of his enrolling at Cal would have been staggering. But he fit in under the "2 percent rule," a policy throughout the state's universities that permitted 2 percent of the entering undergraduates to be admitted at a level below the usual academic entrance requirements. This program was a blessing for the type of student who scratched through high school classes but had the potential to bloom as a student later. In theory, the student with low grades but high learning potential could find a spot in a first-rate university such as Cal and realize his full potential. But in practice, the 2-percenters were often athletes. In Berkeley in 1968, 28 of the 160 freshman 2-percenters were jocks. And Bob was the biggest of the 28.

The academic side of UC was no great problem for him. There were tutors available, people to write term papers, no required attendance in the large lecture halls. And there was always a way to slip somebody into these massive classes to take an exam on his behalf.

Housing was also taken care of for him. Padgett immediately paired Bob with teammate Trent Gaines and Gaines's roommate, Don Hazzard, who'd played on the freshman team a year earlier. Both had been at Berkeley long enough to know their way around. Padgett told Gaines about Bob's Detroit background. "I've been attached to you," Gaines said to Bob when they were introduced. "They're always giving me the *cases*."

Gaines was the sort of black Bob had rarely seen in the atmosphere of Detroit: a flip, jive-talking, confident, secure young man who didn't seem bothered by anything. He was called "Wally Gator," after a smooth-talking cartoon character, and Gaines had a nickname for everyone else; he addressed Bob as either "Stepper" or "Awesome."

Gaines, Hazzard, Bob, and a baseball player named Norman Brown shared a two-bedroom apartment on Blake Street not far off campus. But Bob was at a point he wanted solitude on order. He'd grown up in a crowd in the house in Detroit all those years without having a corner to himself when he needed one. He'd had a little breathing room in junior college and come to covet it; now he was sardined again. He wanted very much to get a place of his own in Berkeley as soon as he could. As much as he often enjoyed the company of his roommates, he frequently couldn't handle their persistent teasing about his size and classes and women. None of their ragging was malicious, but Bob often blew up at Hazzard and Brown. Once he and Brown tangled for several minutes in their room, and the baseball player moved out.

Bob would have, too, but he needed more money to get his own place. As usual, money was the problem. There were plenty of chits from the athletic department for free meals at Larry Blake's Restaurant on Telegraph and at the Durant Hotel. But food chits weren't money. Bob had heard rumors about alumni at big schools slipping athletes plenty of pocket money. He accepted the rumors as truths; he expected this kind of treatment at Berkeley. He didn't ask Padgett. He just expected. Shortly before his move to Berkeley, Bob was given a suit, a pair of shoes, a couple pairs of slacks, and fifty dollars in pocket money—a donation from Cal's Hoop Club, a group of former Berkeley basketball players.

Bob presumed that if he got these gratuities before even showing up at Cal, he'd really see some decent bucks after he arrived in Berkeley. He took it for granted.

"Bob wasn't bought," Padgett said. "He didn't have his hand out. He asked for nothing. He pretty much took care of himself. He resented too much help. He was not a tough guy to please."

Outwardly. But some of the black players who grew close to Presley could sense his persistent depression. "He was lost," said Jackie Ridgle. Jackie was the only Cal basketball player on a big "ride": full gratuities. Most of the others, including Bob, had their tuition and books covered and were given jobs to cover their "subsistence," lodging, meals, and staples. Basketball team leader Russ Critchfield, for example, was paid two dollars an hour to sort clippings in the athletic publicity department. Another player guarded a parking lot. Bob trimmed a section of grass at Cal's Memorial Stadium. On paper, that is. What he did, when he could make it, was report to the football stadium and then immediately check out and be credited with his mandatory number of work hours.

But Ridgle had the deal. Fifty big-school recruiters were after the prep sensation from Altheimer, Arkansas, and so heavy dealing was required. When Jackie came to Berkeley, his mother, sister, and four younger brothers came with him. His sister was accepted at Cal, a job was found for his mother, along with a place for all the Ridgles to live. Jackie also received a 1965 Chevrolet and clothing store discounts. His subsistence "job" was watering a campus lawn. The lawn had an automatic sprinkler system.

Bob and the others knew about Ridgle's ride. They respected a player of his advertised abilities, so they didn't resent his perquisites. But most of them kept hoping that Padgett would come up with something more for them, too. Not that he specifically promised; just that he always sounded so damned positive about how everything would turn out for all of them. On and off the court.

By October Bob wasn't sure he wanted to be a basketball player at Berkeley. Or anywhere else.

During informal workouts and scrimmages in late summer and early fall, he'd begun to doubt his abilities. He knew that now he was in a big league, with big players, players with much more experience than he, players with more intelligence, poise, and physical gifts. His asset was size, and he could see now that size alone wasn't enough. Within a few weeks he'd be facing other big men, better big men. Particularly UCLA's Lew Alcindor, who would change his name to Kareem Abdul-Jabbar after college. Bob knew he could never be as good as Alcindor. But as he read the mounting publicity about himself, he felt that people expected him to perform with near-Alcindor abilities. And what worried him more than anything was that his teammates and possibly Padgett and Herrerias also anticipated this grandeur from him.

He considered himself beaten before he started. He'd been drawn into a trap and knew he'd made no effort to resist. He'd give them only what he felt like giving, nothing more. As far as he was concerned, they weren't giving him much either.

Russ Critchfield was Herrerias's kind of player. A small (five-ten) guard, poised, a leader. Cal's all-time single-season scoring record holder. A second-team all-

American in 1966–67. A cinch all-American this year. A senior, a coach on the floor.

He was called Rusty. He looked like the kid who threw the paper on the porch every dawn. An old-fashioned kind of player who'd been with Russ Messner at Salinas High School. "I always followed what all of my coaches said," said Critchfield. "I don't mean that I was a robot. But I was raised to look upon a coach as the authority figure."

He'd seen Presley briefly at a workout at Hartnell but had not met him. Now Rusty was excited that Bob had come to Cal. "Finally we'd have a big guy at center," he said.

Critchfield wasn't alone in his enthusiasm for the new season to begin. Herrerias himself told a friend, "Presley can make us a contender maybe. He can make it fun to coach." Herrerias had six children and was paid $11,600 that year. He needed fun—and success.

Trent Gaines was eager to get things going, too. He was in a cool mood; he began growing an Afro. It was going to be one helluva season all right.

At the first official practice of the season in Harmon Gymnasium, Herrerias had his players go through finger and hand movements, limbering exercises. Critchfield thought Presley looked heavy; he wondered if Bob was in decent enough shape to withstand Rene's rigorous conditioning program.

Bob flexed his hands and fingers for a few minutes and then walked off the court.

"Get back out here," said Herrerias. His practice sessions were structured. He demanded discipline at every moment of these two-hour workouts. There was no time for interruptions.

"I'm tired, coach," said Bob. "I'll come back when I get a little rest, when I catch my breath."

Critchfield didn't take his eyes off Herrerias. He wondered what the coach was going to do. This was something new. After a pause, Rene told Padgett to talk to Bob, and Padgett sent Gaines.

"C'mon, man," Trent said. "Shake it off and don't mess up. It's too early to be messin' up. Just go back out there and give 'em a little show, Awesome."

There were times when Bob was truly winded by Herrerias's conditioning. And times he was confused by Rene's intricate offensive patterns—all the ball handling, and passing, and rotating, and movement without the ball, and reverse action configurations. Rene did not coach run-and-gun, playground-style basketball; Rene preached a controlled, deliberate offense, one geared to getting the ball to the open man, to making sure the open man was a high percentage shooter, a shooter such as Rusty Critchfield.

It was obvious to Presley, Gaines, and Waddell Blackwell that Rusty was Rene's main man, and so they resented Critchfield, Bob more than the other blacks on the team. Bob saw that if Critchfield was the star, he himself couldn't be. Things weren't turning out quite the way he'd visualized in all those conversations with Padgett. But he did know that Rene, not Padgett, was running this team. And Rusty was Rene's boy. And Rusty was white. Critchfield's whiteness infuriated Bob. He was being deprived. By a white.

Bob couldn't conceal his frustration during practice. If he screwed up an offensive pattern and was criticized by Rene, he'd pout. If he wasn't getting his shots, he'd run to the opposite end of the court and stuff the ball in the basket, even though at that time dunking was not permitted in college basketball. Rene told him to stop dunking, but he'd still do it.

"You could tell all these things bothered Rene," said Critchfield. "He just wasn't used to this kind of thing on one of his teams. None of us who had played for Rene before was prepared for this kind of thing. You could feel the tension building."

Often Bob would tangle under the boards with Wendell Kallenberger, a strong six-six center. Bob called Kallenberger clumsy, accused him of running into him deliberately. Kallenberger was white.

Wayne Stewart, eventually a professional football player, was another Presley sparring partner in basketball scrimmages. Stewart was a six-seven strongman. And white.

"It was obvious Bob didn't like white people," said Critchfield. "We felt a tension with him that we never felt with any of the other black players. I knew there was no way I'd ever understand where he came from. I knew that he couldn't relate to my background either. I never felt that we were enemies, but I guess there was just no way for us to get along."

Athletic director Pete Newell recommended that everybody be patient with Bob. "He just hasn't been around much," Newell said. "It'll take him time to adjust."

And Padgett saw no need for concern. "Every season on every team there are problems, because so many different personalities are involved. Whenever you have twelve individuals together in an intense game like basketball, there are bound to be a few problems."

Bob didn't care if he was looked upon as a problem or not. He didn't want Critchfield as a friend. He didn't care what any of the white players thought about him. He was becoming, by this time, more interested in the

friendship of white women. They could be his ticket to
an easy life.

The women who came to the parties at the apartment
were black. Gaines always tried to pair Bob with a black
woman but couldn't put anything together that lasted
longer than an evening. "Black women are always de-
mandin' too much of you," Bob said. "They wanna be
in control. They wanna run you. First thing you know,
after a couple of nights, they wanna get married. All of
'em are like that."

He told Waddell Blackwell, "White women are just
easier. You can run them."

Bob had his first lengthy experience with a white
woman in Banning. A high school girl, a townie named
Debbie. She'd come up to him after a game, asked if
he was busy, given him her car's description and license
plate number, and told him to meet her in the parking
lot if he was interested. He saw no reason to pass up the
experience. They were together one or two nights a
week, either in her car or his room. There was little
conversation. She'd bring him food sometimes. He hadn't
asked, but mentioned that he never had enough to eat,
so she got the message. Once they drove past a men's
clothing store, and Bob pointed to a shirt in the window
he said he wished he could afford. A few nights later
she brought him the shirt. She was a slender, seventeen-
year-old blonde, not particularly pretty and not very
experienced in bed. He told her what to do, and she did it.

Near the end of his time at Mount San Jacinto, he
started borrowing money from her. He never paid it
back, and she never asked for it. They never had an
actual date, never were in public together. She said
she'd catch hell from her family if she were seen with

him, because Banning was such a small town. Bob said
he might get in trouble at school if they knew he was
going with a white woman. He could have had others,
too; teammates gave him notes with telephone numbers;
girls in class made casual comments with serious implications. He understood that his major attraction was his
basketball stardom, that he was the San Jacinto superstar; he also realized that his blackness was a subsidiary
attraction, that some rebellious young white women
wanted, needed a big black man. When it came time to
move to Berkeley, it wasn't necessary for him to have a
long, mournful conversation with the baby blonde. He
didn't promise to write or call or send for her, and she
didn't ask. The parting was perfunctory. They hadn't
liked each other much.

7

WHITE WOMEN: Bob's roommates all knew about Adriana. She spent as much time in the Blake Street flat as they did, and they used to tease Bob about having her share the rent. They also knew about Sylvia. They knew that when Bob wasn't at Blake Street with Adriana, he was at Sylvia's place in Oakland.

Sylvia appeared first, just after Labor Day. Bob met her walking on Telegraph Avenue. She was a secretary in the English department with a decent salary and a car. A little too intellectual maybe, but Bob wasn't after her books.

Adriana was arranged for him by a mutual friend soon after the season started. Adriana was a bright student, a sorority girl. Neither of the women made any demands on Bob. Neither was particularly attractive. Both were white.

Adriana gradually became the more important of the two. Bob often felt he was an intellectual exercise to the gaunt, stringy Sylvia. She wanted to talk about black culture; he preferred to discuss money. Sylvia gave him about fifty dollars a month, all she could afford. Often she would bring him gifts of jewelry or clothing. All he gave her was his spare time, and he had little of that after Adriana came along. But he didn't drop Sylvia completely; he couldn't afford to. And he never wanted to unload Adriana. Bob thought he was in love with Adriana Wheeler.

She was a twenty-year-old sophomore, dark-haired, short, rather chunky, the daughter of a navy captain based in Italy. She was the oldest of five children and had been a mother's helper. Despite all the moves because of her father's transfers, she had done well in schools in Nevada, New Mexico, Rhode Island, and California. Adriana pictured herself as "the ideal little kid." Although her father frequently, and stridently, disciplined her younger brothers and sisters, Adriana felt his wrath only once. She was sixteen and enjoying high school in Orange County, California, when the navy ordered her father to San Diego. She told her parents she wanted to stay in Orange County with friends, that they could leave without her. "I'm sick of moving," she said. She locked herself in her room and refused to speak to anybody. Her father finally broke in, flung Adriana against a wall, and thrashed her. She eventually moved to San Diego and then overseas with the rest of the Wheelers.

Italy was not unpleasant. She found an old high school boyfriend near Naples. She traveled. She learned Italian and took a job in an art store. In 1966 and early 1967, while her father cruised various Mediterranean ports and her mother followed, Adriana was housemother to her brothers and sisters. When her parents returned to Naples after several months, she told them she'd like to return to California for college. She'd read about the growing hippie movement in the Bay Area, and Berkeley sounded exciting. Both her mother and father had attended Cal, but they said they didn't want her in the "flower child" atmosphere there. Any other college was fine with them.

"I'll join a sorority," she said. "What can happen in a sorority?" She convinced them the sorority house would protect her from the hazards of a hippie love-in, and finally they bent.

Gamma Phi Beta pledged her in the fall of 1967, and she soon fell into the routine of neophyte sorority life: mixers and beer busts with fraternities, heavy study load, the subservient chores of a pledge. Only the social aspects were bothersome. Adriana didn't feel she fit with the fraternity types. She was insecure at the parties and drank too much and found herself in the bedroom of a guy she barely knew. "They laughed at me and called me names," she said. "They didn't believe I didn't want to mess around." And she didn't. At the time Adriana met Bob Presley, she was a virgin.

She first saw him at a basketball game in early December. His physical attraction was unmistakable to her. She just *had* to go out with him. She found someone at the sorority house who knew someone who knew someone who knew Bob Presley, and a meeting in the Bear's Lair, a campus hangout, was arranged, with another couple present.

Both were nervous and talked very little at their first meeting. Bob suggested she meet him outside Harmon Gym after the next game, and she was delighted with the invitation. He borrowed a car and they drove up to Grizzly Peak Boulevard, in the Berkeley hills, to kiss and talk, but mostly talk. From that moment, they were nearly inseparable for almost seven months. Adriana was fascinated by his celebrity, size, and blackness, and she was not entirely certain what drew Bob to her. He'd regularly pick her up at the Gamma Phi house after complaining that she wanted to be seen with him only because he was a basketball star. "You just want to exploit our relationship," he said. "You're tryin' to show me off." And in the first weeks that was true. Adriana was flattered that a campus bigshot like Bob would want to spend so much time with her. She was surprised he wasn't already tied down to other, more attractive women. She didn't know about Sylvia.

Their early dates involved only sorority functions. She was dazzled when he rented a Cadillac to take her to a big Gamma Phi dance. Everything about him—his silk underpants, his cologne, his love of jazz, his brooding blackness—tantalized her. And Adriana began to see that Bob was obsessed with her. For a full month he treated her with courteous affection. They listened to music on Blake Street; then he'd take her back to the sorority house and kiss her good night. Finally he said he had to go to bed with her, and Adriana didn't resist.

By the third month of their relationship, he was beating her regularly.

The first beating came when they were alone in the Blake flat one afternoon. They had sex, and then, arguing over an imagined slight, he uncoiled a coat hanger and struck her on an arm. His eyes were like a robot's. He said nothing. He just hit and hit, and then in a moment he stopped. And cried.

"Forgive me," he said. "Please forgive me. I can't help myself."

"He'd always cry after he beat me," Adriana said. "He'd always ask my forgiveness. I thought he was really sorry."

As the beatings persisted, Adriana tried to figure out why she didn't break off the relationship. "I'm probably masochistic," she told a friend, "but, honest to God, I don't enjoy getting beaten like that. It hurts. And most of the time I really, really cry. But I'm never actually frightened. I never want to get up and run away. This may sound silly, but I don't think it's anything personal."

She didn't think the beatings were sexual. "I never get off on them," she said, "and I don't think Bob does either. His sexual tastes don't run to beatings. Maybe he's just attacking my whiteness. Maybe that's the only thing it's about."

She covered her welts and scars with long sleeves or slacks. Only once did Bob hit her in the face, and there was no way she could hide the black eye from her sorority sisters. She lied about the injury, but not all the women believed her.

Adriana was the white world, one Bob didn't understand except that he knew it was richer and better off. The only way he could deal with it was to be part of it; basketball could make him part of it, but that seemed so much trouble and time. He couldn't use ball the way he was using Adriana and Sylvia and, if he wanted, other white women. Ball was work—working for somebody else, for somebody rich and white who would profit from his work. He had watched his mother and father work for whites for years, and what did it get them? Same thing it would get him. Nothin'.

The Presleys had never had it easy and never would have it easy. Not unless Bob could figure out something: a way to have whites work for him.

It was done. He'd seen it done in Detroit. He'd heard about and seen the black pimps with their white stables.

Plenty of 'em. The blacks who had the good life in
Detroit were the pimps. They had cars, money, and
clothes. They used whites, white girls and white tricks.
They knew what they were doing and did it easily.

There were many pimps in Detroit, but only a few at
Cal. A little quiet action in Berkeley, down in the flats,
and much more activity over in Oakland, but not so
much that there wasn't room for another good pimp
with a good stable, a white stable. Bob heard about the
Robinson brothers, the three leading pimps in the Eastbay. He'd met one of the Robinsons after a game,
smoked some dope in the man's Caddy, answered questions about ball. Nothing sinister. A leading pimp could
tell his friends he was tight with Cal's basketball star.
And Bob, if he wished, could ask Julius Robinson for
a freebie date. One night Julius drove Bob around his
locations along San Pablo and Grove and West Mac-
Arthur in Oakland, pointing with pride to his girls on
his corners. Bob was impressed.

"Got the prime spots, huh?"

"Not much competition," Robinson said. "We don't
encourage competition."

"You mean you'd make trouble if I went out and got
a license of my own?" Bob laughed.

"Just check me first," Julius said. "Always glad to
help a friend. But there are friends, and there are
friends."

"I'll keep that in mind," said Bob. And he did.

He mentioned his conversation with Robinson one
afternoon as he and Sylvia sat in the grass in front of
Sproul Hall. He told her both of them could make a
few bucks if she didn't mind doing that sort of thing. He
was lighthearted; he wasn't sure himself if he was
serious. And he was glad when Sylvia refused to answer

directly and changed the subject. He sensed virgin territory here, in more ways than one.

He didn't even discuss the Robinsons with Adriana. He was not sure where he stood with her. He wanted her so badly; he couldn't lose her.

Bob was relieved to see the Cal basketball season start. If he had to go through any more of those run, run, run preseason practices, he would have quit. But Padgett continued to reassure him he'd have a great year. Even Herrerias told a writer, "Presley should be Cal's best offensive center in twelve years. I'm very pleased with the progress Bob has made and the way he has adapted to our situation."

Late in the preseason, Rene developed more plays built around Bob. The coach didn't want to squander the height, and with an outside (Critchfield) and inside (Presley) offensive attack, the Bears could be tough to defend against. Bob was beginning to believe that Critchfield might not be the whole show after all, and on those days when Bob did give his all in a scrimmage, Critchfield enjoyed playing with him. "If he uses his talent, he's really something," said Rusty.

Critchfield dislocated a shoulder in the home opener against Idaho on December 2, 1967. The scoring burden immediately fell to Bob, who responded with eighteen points and sixteen rebounds in a Cal victory. A very impressive beginning.

After the game, Bob surprised Critchfield by coming over to the training table where Rusty was being treated. "We need you," Bob told him. "Get well quick."

"I really appreciate that," said Critchfield. He could see that Bob was glowing with confidence over his performance. And relaxed. Critchfield was stunned that

Presley had spoken to him, for the first time in all those months, with a degree of sincerity.

Critchfield sat out the next three games. In one of them, against St. Mary's, Bob grabbed twenty-seven rebounds for a single-game Cal record. He was dominating, and he was surprised at how easy it all was; perhaps he'd misjudged this level of competition. Maybe he *was* good enough.

Even after Rusty returned, Presley was the prevailing figure as the Bears won seven of their first eight. Bob averaged eighteen rebounds, shooting 56 percent from the field and scoring an average of twenty-four points, including a one-game high of thirty-three. There was speculation that Bob might eventually erase Critchfield's scoring record, that Cal might actually give UCLA trouble in the conference, that Bob was another Alcindor.

By December's end, Critchfield was completely healthy again. In the final two games of the year he scored sixty-four points. Bob had good numbers in those games too, but Rusty was edging back into the spotlight. Cal now had a solid one-two scoring punch. Herrerias was having his fun. As was Bob. His celebrity had come so quickly, he was getting light-headed, often as loose as Gaines. Bob decided he'd start working on an Afro, too.

Nobody had said anything about Trent's, so Bob figured nobody cared. Hell, the way the team was going, he could grow horns and nobody would object.

Cal's conference season began in Corvallis, Oregon, on January 5, 1968, against a low-rated Oregon State team. Bob had to face a novice seven-foot center named Vic Bartolome. The Bears figured to romp.

But the Oregon State coach, in a surprising ploy, had a six-five forward guard the five-ten Critchfield, and

Rusty couldn't score his usual number of points. Presley hit for twenty-three—not enough, as Cal fell by seven. Bob was shoved around on offense and raged at the officials, but Herrerias refused to criticize the refereeing.

Next day, down at Eugene, Oregon, Critchfield scored thirty-six and Bob twenty-nine as Cal easily defeated Oregon. Presley was called six times for goaltending infractions and continued to rail at the refs. But he made quite an impression on Oregon coach Steve Belko. "Presley presents the same problems as Alcindor," said Belko. "He has the touch, he's active, he takes so much away from you on defense."

Bob was getting swept up by the competition. He played with far more aggression than he thought he could manage. He didn't worry about his goaltending problems, but he did wonder why the refs always seemed to make calls against him. "I'm learning to always expect the worst from them," he said.

Now, though, it was time to expect Alcindor. The next game, six days away, was in Berkeley. Against UCLA.

He told Adriana not to talk to him about Alcindor or the upcoming game. "I don't want to think about it," he said. She thought he looked very worried.

The Bruins worried everybody in basketball. They were coming to Berkeley with forty-four consecutive victories and their entire collegiate championship team of the previous year intact. Alcindor was still only a junior, listed at seven-one and a half. A Cal press release that week called Alcindor "the ultimate test for Cal's very effective big man, Bob Presley" and cited their current statistics. Alcindor at that point was ranked tenth nationally in total scoring, Presley eighteenth. But Bob had outrebounded the Bruin thus far that season.

"There's going to be a lot of pressure on you this week," Padgett told Bob. "Tremendous pressure. Try to ignore it. Do the best you can in the game. That's all you can do; take it in stride. This isn't a suicidal situation. Don't make this game a personal thing. Don't take on personal responsibility for the whole world." Padgett hadn't any idea whether Bob could emotionally handle a game like this. It might be too soon for him to be in this kind of spotlight. "But there's no place now for him to hide," Padgett said.

Critchfield sensed that Bob was tighter than usual in that week's practice sessions. Herrerias had them work on a special defense, a match-up zone, in hopes of holding Alcindor to a reasonable number of points. Rene had decided on the zone defense because he felt Presley might be too pressured playing Alcindor one-on-one. But during one of the workouts Bob told the coach, "Hey, man, I can handle Big Lew. I'm sure I can take care of him. Lemme go on him alone, huh?"

"Rene liked Bob's confidence," said Critchfield, "and so did the rest of us. We thought we might be able to beat UCLA in that game. We thought we might be able to win the conference championship. But still, in the back of my mind I knew there'd be an awful lot of pressure on Bob. He was getting so much ink, and all that ink makes for big pressure."

But the ink flowing around the game had been diminished by a strike at the two San Francisco daily newspapers, and so *Oakland Tribune* sportswriter Dave Newhouse had the pregame flourishes almost to himself. He arranged an interview with Bob; he wanted Bob to talk about Alcindor.

Newhouse always felt intimidated by Presley. Even after a big performance, Bob appeared reluctant to speak with him. Newhouse, a white, didn't know how to

approach the big black. He often thought of not bothering to get quotes from Bob after a game. "I always felt
he had a mean instinct," Newhouse said. "I wondered if
he was a good person." Newhouse was too young, too
new at the job to be cynical or contemptuous about
athletes. And he did not consider himself to be bigoted.
He just couldn't figure a way to get close to Bob.

"I'd watch him closely in games to try and get a handle
on him, find specific things to ask him about later,"
Newhouse said. "I'd sometimes get the impression that
he was happy at Cal, but then other times I had the
feeling that he was a lost person. Somebody who didn't
have control of himself."

Presley told Newhouse that he'd have no trouble
guarding Alcindor by himself. "I'll save my team thirty-
three points. You'll see," Bob promised. "You put one
man on Lew and he'll score twenty-five, but double-team
him and he'll get fifty-eight." Newhouse wasn't sure if
he was being put on, but at least he had Presley talking;
the reporter was so nervous in Presley's presence that he
didn't perceive Bob's nervousness.

"I sure hope the coach lets me play Lew one-on-one,"
said Bob. "I think that's the only way to play him. I can
play him; I can jump with him. Alcindor's great, sure,
and I give him the respect he deserves. He's better than
I am, but I won't duck out."

Eventually Newhouse asked him about the Cal team,
about how he enjoyed playing with Russ Critchfield.
Bob hid the frown, hid it well. "I just wish that Russ
and I were both sophomores and had three years together. That little man wins games for us."

Newhouse had enough and was glad it was over. Bob
was sorry it ever started. All the sportswriters ever talked
about was bullshit. What the hell did these bullshit white
sportswriters know? "I keep waitin' for them to ask one

question," Bob said. "Just one question: 'To what, Mister Presley, do you owe your success?' And you know what I'd answer? Two words. I'd tell 'em, 'Billie Holiday,' then I'd walk away and let them figure it out."

"You ready, man?" Gaines asked while they changed in the locker room. "You gonna be awesome, Awesome, against the big L.A. from big L.A.?"

"He'll get his points," Bob conceded, "but I'll get mine, too."

Waddell Blackwell had the impression Bob was up for this challenge. And if he wasn't, he was covering very well.

Alcindor hit his first two shots. Bob fouled him twice. Alcindor sank four free throws. Herrerias called a time-out, and in the huddle around the Cal bench Bob bellowed, "Hey, you guys aren't helping me out."

Soon after the time-out, Presley connected on a three-point play to tie the game at eight, but then Alcindor took total command. He made four consecutive baskets, and gradually UCLA pulled away to a halftime lead of 52–37. The Bears were not shooting well, although they did not play incompetently. Bob managed to make a couple of baskets over Alcindor and even blocked three of his shots. Bob did not embarrass himself; indeed, he'd had thirteen points and thirteen rebounds. But Alcindor finished with forty-four points, a Harmon Gym record, and seventeen rebounds.

"No college player can stop Lew one-on-one," said UCLA coach John Wooden. "I'm tickled to death Cal played him like that. I think Presley did a reasonably good job. We expected him to be good, and he was. Lew did miss fifteen shots, and I think Presley's presence had something to do with that."

And Bob's own coach was equally considerate. "Presley played Lew as well as can be expected," Herrerias said, "but Bob was facing the best."

Nick Peters, sports editor of the *Berkeley Gazette*, was the only sportswriter with whom Bob had any rapport, perhaps because Peters was at Harmon Gym almost as often as the team. Or perhaps because Peters was nonchalant and didn't ask questions just for the sake of asking questions. And Peters would sometimes talk about matters other than basketball. Peters was white—all the sportswriters were—but Bob never built barriers with Peters.

"Both coaches are saying very nice things about how you played tonight," Nick said. "Wooden was high on you."

"Well, I wasn't good enough," Bob replied. "Hell, it seemed like Lew got fifty off me. And he could have blocked every shot I took if he really wanted to. It's like he's bigger than seven-one and a half. And one more thing; next time before we play UCLA, don't be runnin' my numbers and Alcindor's together."

Peters had never seen Bob so discouraged. He told Presley to shrug it off. "You'll bounce back tomorrow night," he said. And Peters drove downtown to the *Gazette* office and wrote the game story and locker room story, the latter headlined with the words "Presley Dejected Loser."

Bob told Gaines that the loss was Critchfield's fault. "Damn Critchfield tryin' to do everything himself. I'd be open, and he'd never pass to me. Damn Critchfield wasn't doin' a thing to help out."

The next evening, against Southern California, Bob missed twelve of eighteen shots as seven-one center Ron Taylor fronted him constantly and prevented the Bears from getting the ball to Presley. But Bob was not hustling or trying to get himself open. He played raggedly, as did nearly everyone on the team except Critchfield.

"Taylor beat Presley everywhere," Herrerias told Nick Peters. "Taylor doesn't have an awful lot of tools, but he worked hard and he got the job done. I guess we were flat after playing UCLA. But that's no excuse."

Among the spectators that night was Bob Feerick, general manager of the professional San Francisco Warriors, one of the first National Basketball Association executives to assess Presley's capabilities. "You see hundreds just like him in the ghetto playgrounds," Feerick said. "He's a dog. He's big, but he doesn't hustle. He's strong, but he doesn't have the mentality to become a good basketball player, or really a good anything. Because he won't sacrifice his body or his outside interests to play the game the way it should be played. Because he doesn't have the dedication to do what's necessary to make the team."

Feerick's appraisal, coupled with repercussions of the events of the next few weeks, became Bob Presley's résumé for the balance of his basketball life.

8

GAINES BORROWED A car from Padgett after the USC game and convinced Presley to ride down to Long Beach with him. Trent hadn't been home since Christmas, and Bob had been with him then, too. The Gaineses were a close, warm family; Bob enjoyed their company and Mrs. Gaines's cooking. He appreciated the Gaineses' instant acceptance of him.

During the drive they talked about the team, the games they'd lost. Bob repeatedly criticized Critchfield. "Rene lets him dominate too much," Bob said. "All the plays are designed for Critchfield. There's no gravy left for the rest of us."

"Lookee here, Awesome," replied Gaines, "Rusty is a good ballplayer. You can't take anything away from him."

"But he's such a damn selfish mother."

"Rene lets him free-lance. He does what the coach wants him to do. If Rene told him to play another way, he'd play another way."

102

"Damn white coach just wants to make his white star look good all the time," said Bob.

Trent turned up the car radio. He didn't want to pursue this line with Bob; he'd already said over and over: "You don't trust nobody. For no reason at all, man, you think everybody's always on your case. You got the biggest persecution complex I've ever seen. If you can't dig how to mellow out, you're gonna be a real case, Awesome. A real bad case."

They arrived in Long Beach in time for a large, companionable breakfast at Trent's house and planned to loaf and sleep the rest of the day and into the evening. They were in no hurry to get back up to Berkeley. Trent's mother teased him about his Afro; he'd tried to plaster it down for the UCLA and USC games, televised in Southern California, so he wouldn't catch hell from his mother. "I've just got a half-Afro," Trent said, "but Awesome here has the real thing—an Afro dizzyact."

They returned to Berkeley by early Tuesday afternoon, well before practice. Both had been late to a practice a few weeks earlier; Rene had not made a big issue out of it, but he did advise them never to be late again. Practices were important. Games could be won and lost by the developments in practice sessions.

Bob and Trent were tired by the long drive. Bob didn't feel like running in the gym for an hour and a half. "Let's just cool it today, huh?" he said. Trent agreed. While the rest of the team was at the gym, Bob and Trent napped on Blake Street.

Before practice began Wednesday afternoon, Herrerias called Trent aside and asked where he'd been Tuesday. Gaines told him the truth. "I was thinking about starting you against Portland Saturday, but now I can't," the coach said.

"I can understand that," Trent replied. Herrerias didn't ask him why Bob had missed practice, nor did Trent mention him.

Bob told Herrerias he'd been tied up in court on Tuesday afternoon working out payment of a traffic ticket. Herrerias asked for details, and Bob tried to bluff. When the coach checked out the story and discovered the lie, he told Bob he'd been suspended from the team. Indefinitely; perhaps for the balance of the season.

On his way out of the gym, Bob told one of the black football players that he'd been thrown off the team for growing an Afro.

"Man don't like black hair," Bob said. "Man don't like blacks period."

Herrerias had had a haircut rule in previous seasons, but this year he had not bothered to emphasize it. "If I asked Bob to get a haircut, it was so long ago I don't remember. His haircut definitely was not a reason for the suspension."

On Friday afternoon Bob couldn't reach Padgett, who was in Los Angeles on a recruiting visit. He sent word to Herrerias that he wanted the suspension lifted. His message: "All I want is to go to school and play ball." But Herrerias already had another message that day, via representatives of the UC chancellor. They had met with athletic director Pete Newell. The chancellor's office did not want to risk racial trouble if Presley weren't reinstated. By Friday's end, Presley was reinstated.

Bob had lunch with the team Saturday. The suspension was not discussed. He was advised he had to sit out that night's game against Portland and then could rejoin the team. That evening Bob sat in the bleachers at Harmon, scrawled autographs, did an interview on campus radio, and watched Cal win 74–61 behind Critchfield's twenty-four points. Gaines appeared as a sub and scored eight points.

Reporters tried to get Herrerias to discuss the Presley situation, but Rene had nothing to say. The coach's demeanor was described by several writers as "sullen."

Bob, on the other hand, was ebullient after the reinstatement. Adriana had never seen him so high. He told her Herrerias didn't like his haircut, and when she insisted she heard he was suspended because he missed practice, Bob still held to the haircut excuse. "You just want to believe the coach is prejudiced," she said. "You're always misunderstanding things. You're looking for things that aren't there."

"It was the haircut, damn it. That's what some of the boys on the street say, and that's what I say. He bounced me 'cause of the Afro."

"Well," she answered, "whatever it was, you're sure getting lots more attention now." She could tell he was very pleased with all this attention. She wondered how long it would last. On Monday, Adriana had her answer. On Monday, all of the team's white players quit the squad.

Cal didn't have another game scheduled until February 2, so there was no practice on Monday, January 22. At the urging of team manager Pat Gilligan, a team meeting was called for four o'clock that afternoon in Harmon Gym. At least two of the black players, Waddell Blackwell and Clarence Johnson, were invited to the meeting but declined to attend.

"It wasn't just one person who led us into the walkout," said Critchfield. "It was just something that we all kind of talked about—the fact that Rene had suspended Bob for a good reason, and now Rene had been forced to reinstate him. We didn't think that was fair to Rene."

The white players and team manager Gilligan talked for nearly six hours. A statement was prepared:

We the undersigned members of the UC basketball team are taking this necessary action involving our participation in California athletics. Last week, Coach Rene Herrerias took disciplinary action dismissing a player, an action which he felt was for the betterment of the team. Two years ago, three players were dismissed for similar reasons and the judgment of the coach was considered valid. We respect Coach Herrerias's right to make any decision regarding the team's welfare and expect these decisions to be further respected by the University and the University community.

However, such is not the case. The final action of reinstating the dismissed player was a result of pressures from University administrators and implications brought out in a meeting thereof. We feel these implications and pressures have no place on the basketball court and until such pressures are unconditionally removed, we cannot participate in California basketball.

Critchfield said that guidance toward framing the statement came from Bob Tannenbaum, a third-year law student and former Cal assistant basketball coach. "When I stop to think about it," said Critchfield, "what we should have done was all sit down and hash the thing out rather than issue that statement. Everybody had things bottled up inside them. If we could have talked about it, all of us together, we could have worked things out. But the way we did it, everything got out of hand."

Quickly. As soon as the white players struck, the black athletes counterattacked. They demanded the firing of Herrerias and two white assistant football coaches. They issued a laundry list of grievances.

And out front was the big man. "The racial problem

has been here for a long time," Presley said at a news conference. "One reason I was suspended was my refusal to cut my hair. I'd just like to continue my education and play basketball."

"Somebody's really using Presley," said athletic director Pete Newell. "Outsiders are coming on campus and using him. This haircut thing has become a cause."

"Nobody could see how this thing would end," said Padgett. "Nobody had any idea how it would all turn out."

It turned out well for Padgett. He maintained he had no impact on the result, and most of those close to the situation agree with him, even several who didn't like the man. Then there are a few persons who detested Jim Padgett; they will always contend that his fine hand was behind events that brought down Rene Herrerias.

"During that whole business, Bob never complained to me. Nor would I have allowed him to do that," said Padgett. "Rene didn't ask my opinion, nor should he have. Pete Newell told me to stay where I was. Pete said to me, 'The last thing we need is another opinion.' Nobody asked my opinion. I had no magic wand. I had no authority. I just did what I was told—and I was told not to do anything. It was a tense, strange time."

It didn't seem as though anyone was in the middle. Not even the two newspapermen covering this first significant incident of racial turmoil in a major school sports program. The *Oakland Tribune*'s Newhouse continued to feel uncomfortable trying to talk to Presley and focused mainly on the white players' case and the athletic department's point of view. "I'm not happy with my coverage," he said, "but maybe I'm just used to trusting the 'official' side of the story."

But the *Berkeley Gazette*'s Peters leaned in the other direction. "I feel the black athletes are completely justified in complaining about requests to change their physical appearance—like trimming the popular natural haircuts," he wrote. "It's a matter of fact that the clean-cut, crew-cut youngster best exemplifies athletics to the warped minds of some coaches. . . ."

And Peters persistently defended Presley. He called him "insecure" and "an unharnessed cage talent" and said, "Perhaps people expected too much of the big Bear. . . . I hold the utmost respect for him because he honestly wants to better the situation. The fact he's a talented basketball player should have no bearing on his awareness of basic issues that torment most bright, young Negroes."

The man who ran Berkeley's Black Students Union, Frank Jenkins, disagreed; he felt that the only issue Presley believed in, and was tormented by, was the issue of Bob Presley. But he wasn't unhappy to see so much fuss being made over an Afro haircut, "even though it was such a secondary issue," he said.

Jenkins, a hulking, beefy black with an incongruous high-pitched voice, was recruited to Cal as a football tackle from Oakland's Laney Junior College in 1966. Blacks were as scarce on the Cal football team as they'd been on the basketball squad. Jenkins played a soul music station on his portable radio in the locker room; an assistant coach told him it was OK to listen to that music if he was in the locker room alone but to turn off the radio when others came in. The year Jenkins enrolled at Berkeley there were only 226 black students on campus. "And a lot of them were Africans," he said. "Sometimes I'd go a whole week without seeing a black woman." Early on, he joined the Afro-American Student

Association, eventually known as the Black Students Union. He quit the football team after two months and concentrated on classes and black activism; with the Economic Opportunity Program and the 2-percent policy now in effect, hundreds more blacks were on campus by the time he became president of the BSU.

When the Presley case broke, Jenkins wasn't the only black activist on campus. Harry Edwards, outspoken in the matter of injustice toward black athletes at nearby San Jose State University, came to one of Jenkins's BSU meetings. "He wanted to get maximum publicity mileage out of this," said Jenkins. "We turned him down." Also on the periphery of the Presley fuss was a black activist Oakland attorney named Donald Warden, who later had business dealings with Bob.

"Everybody tried to make this a Bob Presley incident," said Jenkins, "but all Bob wanted to do was talk about his hair."

There was a major press conference at which the black athletes made their demands for increased aid, tutoring, and summer jobs. Jenkins wanted football player Bobby Smith, the team's best black, to be the spokesman. "I told Presley to keep quiet at this thing," said Jenkins, "but as soon as the TV people turned on their lights, he started talking. He wanted all the attention. His biggest enemy in the world was himself."

Wayne Brooks, another black football player, pitied Presley during the weeks of strife. "He was a mound of clay, shaped, designed, and fashioned by those around him. If he hadn't been so big, maybe he wouldn't have been such a center of attention—or wanted to be," said Brooks. "There were so many people telling him what to do all the time this thing was going on. People who wanted him to revolt, 'cause if he did all the other blacks on campus would fall in line. And he took all this advice. He accepted the advice to be accepted himself."

Jenkins and Brooks hoped to see Cal's athletic establishment, particularly the football program, brought down. And they knew the Presley case could be the catalyst.

"Most of us black football players had been lied to when we were recruited," said Brooks. "The year I came here there were three black players from South Carolina on our team who thought they were at UCLA. You can figure out what kind of recruiting job was done on them."

Tannenbaum, the law student, the former assistant basketball coach, attacked Presley and the 2-percent rule after the black athletes attacked the athletic department.

"It will be a tragedy for civil rights," said Tannenbaum, "if these false accusations [by black athletes] are incorporated. . . . For justice to be done, the truth must be made perfectly clear so that a valid determination of the issues can be reached. Presley was suspended solely for disciplinary reasons. He constantly violated team discipline by not undergoing conditioning exercises, by referring to the coach derogatorily, by hostility toward his teammates, and by not attending practice."

Tannenbaum said that Presley, Ridgle, and several other black basketball players "have gained access into the university as a result of the 2-percent program. These students are unable to survive at the University academically. They have received tutoring . . . their courses have been selected assuming they're the easiest courses available."

And team manager Gilligan also had a statement on behalf of the white basketball players. He, Critchfield, and another white player had met with Newell and Herrerias, and now Gilligan said that the white players would return to the squad if a university spokesman admitted Herrerias was *forced* to reinstate Presley, if Herrerias was given full authority to run the team, and if the black players ceased their charges of racism. Gilligan said that the white players would play "if there's no team disillusionment or coach disillusionment." The team, he said, could play with or without Presley. "We've had some great practices without him."

Then the black athletes had joint statements of their own. They also threatened not to play. Emerging as spokesman for the black athletes was the football team's defensive back Bobby Smith, judged by blacks and whites as one of the outstanding players in the West at his position. It was assumed, on the Berkeley campus at least, that Smith had a future in professional football. But once he became the official spokesman for Cal's black athletes, once he drew the attention of the sporting press and the electronic media, Smith became noted more for his brief sign of militancy than for his ability to defend against the forward pass, and he was not drafted by any team in the National Football League. Some pro scouts said Smith simply lacked the size and strength to compete on that level; his friends insisted he was bad-mouthed because of his posture following the Presley incident.

Smith said the black athletes had a lengthy bill of particulars illustrating their treatment by the athletic department as second-class citizens. The grievances, said Smith, were both practical and emotional.

"On numerous occasions, our personal and physical

appearance have been ridiculed by members of the athletic department, and in at least one case has led directly to the suspension of a black athlete."

The blacks on campus who believed that Presley had been suspended because of his Afro haircut could not fathom that such a fuss was being made over something so petty. Facial hair was as much a problem for the black athlete in the 1960s as the Afro. Coaches saw beards, moustaches, or long sideburns as a sign of player revolt. To a coach, a clean-shaven appearance meant a well-disciplined athlete. But the blacks fancied facial hair, felt it gave them an air of distinction in tandem with their hip clothing. A beard did not make them less a dribbler or shooter or pass catcher or curve ball hitter; the blacks were dumbfounded that their coach believed more hair made for less athletic productivity. It was as if college recruiters expected their black athletes to turn middle-class white once enrolled.

Then there was "personal appearance," their style of dress. The black, particularly the black athlete who traveled and had the opportunity to compare styles, not to mention the spare time on the road to browse in shops, was always one step ahead of his white counter- part: in tailored jeans, in leathers, in suedes, in silk shirts, in flared trousers. The conservative white coach of the 1960s, then making an adjustment to a garment as flashy as a double-knit sportscoat, wondered if his black players were posing as a sartorial circus; there was no discipline to what most coaches then viewed as far-out fashions. Peacockery was not part of the game. Then. By the mid-1970s, some college basketball coaches dressed with more flash than their players, black or white. Three-piece suits were as common as folding chairs to a basketball arena sideline. And by the time coaches and white players started to dress like "dudes," the black players had switched to a more conservative fashion bent—and shorter hair styles.

Bobby Smith also raised grievances on the practical level. "In spite of promises to the contrary," he said, "after having been recruited, black athletes are left to fend for themselves in finding housing without appropriate support from the athletic department. . . . The assumption is made that black athletes are poor students and are lacking in intelligence, the result being that we receive inferior academic advice and counseling." Smith said that several coaches lacked competence in handling the individual problems of black athletes.

Presley and Waddell Blackwell read the account of Smith's news conference in the *Berkeley Gazette* the next day. They lounged in Waddell's flat on Bonita Street, pulled on a bottle of Boone's Farm loganberry wine, and decided that most of the grievances came from the black football players. "We got it easy on the basketball team compared to them," Waddell said.

"Listen," said Bob, "I got more academic advice and counseling than I got time to bother with. Thing is, there ain't as many of us to worry about as there is football players. But that don't make it right either."

Blackwell believed he could be more objective about the status of the black athlete at Cal than his black basketball teammates, or the black football players, could. Waddell had both an athletic scholarship and a basketball grant. He came to Cal as much to learn as to play ball; he wanted a degree more than a pro basketball contract. Although Waddell spent most of his free time with Presley, he had been around black players on both the basketball and football teams often enough to realize that academics didn't interest most of them. "A lot of guys," he said to Bob, "don't see the importance of school or studying. They just don't pay attention to what's going on in the classroom." He agreed that there probably weren't enough tutors available for all of the black football players who may have wanted the help, but he shared Bob's feeling about the availability of tutors for the basketball team. "We have as many as we need," he said. He was convinced, too, that Herrerias was concerned about his players' grades. "Rene wants you to graduate," he said, "and the main thing Padgett wants is for you to stay eligible."

"Hell," said Presley, "from what I hear, the damn football coaches don't really give a shit about the black players anyway." He agreed with another of Bobby Smith's contentions, that the black football players were given worse working conditions and pay than the whites for summer and scholarship-earning jobs.

"If you're white, all right; if you're brown, hang around; but if you're black, go back." Presley laughed as he paraphrased the folk song. "I'm just glad," he said, "I ain't no linebacker."

"Even if you wanted to be, you couldn't be," said Waddell. "Bobby's bitchin' about that stuff, too. The coaches take a black guy who maybe was a good quarter-back at his high school and make him into a defensive back. They want people they think are smart to play quarterback and linebacker and those places. And they don't think we're smart enough."

"They just don't put us in enough snap courses," Bob said. "We need more courses like Public Speaking 1A."

Now Waddell laughed. Public Speaking 1A was the current snap course for athletes at Cal. The instructor actually recruited black athletes because he was, in the late 1960s, doing research on a book about black rage. He assigned speech topics he felt would embellish his research, and as long as a student followed that topic, a high passing grade was sure to follow.

"There's an easier course around if you can get in it," said Waddell. "English for Foreign Students."

One black basketball player at Cal did manage to enroll in that course in his freshman year. His Southern accent may have led the instructor to believe he indeed was a foreigner. The player was the only student in the class that term who spoke English. He passed without benefit of a tutor.

One of the key demands listed by Bobby Smith called for hiring minority coaches. "We feel that the university, in light of its commitment to liberalism, should make a sincere effort to accomplish that," Smith said. Smith's phrase "commitment to liberalism" was his most effective; it hit a nerve. UC-Berkeley had made a well-publicized, unflagging philosophic commitment to liberalism; the campus was the locus of liberalism in the academic community.

But UC chancellor Roger W. Heyns wanted to keep the "haircut" problem from exploding into more volatile issues. Bob Presley, without really trying, had become a remarkable Cause, and Berkeley already was a magnet for Causes.

To cool things momentarily, Heyns appointed a committee to investigate the state of Cal's sports program. Heyns empowered his committee to gather facts, hear grievances, make recommendations.

Herrerias induced the white players to return to practice by publicly announcing, at a press conference they requested he call, that it was his decision alone to reinstate Presley. "I also give the team complete assurance that I will make all decisions regarding the basketball team on my own." He also said he didn't think there was any racial dissension on the team.

The "reunion" game, on February 2, was lost at the Air Force Academy. Presley, Gaines, and Blackwell scored only seven points combined. Critchfield was under his average with only eighteen. "The season was shot by the strike," he said. "After the strike was over, I didn't feel like playing too much anymore. In fact, I walked out of practice one day not long after we all came back to the team. I told Rene I wasn't gonna play anymore. But Pete Newell said I had a responsibility to Rene, to my teammates, and to the university. So I stayed on the team. But basketball wasn't fun after that."

Critchfield was one of the players interviewed by the chancellor's fact-finding committee. "From their questions, I had the feeling they were trying to make Rene the scapegoat," he said, "but I held Rene in the highest regard. Maybe I was too much in awe of him, and of Pete Newell, too. In a way, I guess, I loved Rene because he was my coach. I would have lain down on the freeway for him if he'd asked me."

At a practice session soon after the strike ended, Critchfield threw a pass to Presley in the post. The pass was off target, and Presley couldn't handle it. "Don't ever throw a pass at me like that again," Bob stormed.

"I'll never throw you a pass again at all," said Critchfield.

All they could do was play out the season. The night after the Air Force loss, Cal defeated Denver. Then a week later Herrerias benched Bob because Presley was unable, for reasons of his own, to learn some new plays

Rene installed for the game against Washington. After eight minutes of that game, Washington led 14–13. Herrerias sent in Presley, and quickly Bob and Gaines shot Cal into the lead. At one point Bob made nine straight free throws. And it was apparent he was familiar with the new plays—when he wanted to run them. But much of the time in that game he merely wandered from one side of the foul lane to the other, waiting to be passed the ball. Herrerias refused to discuss Bob's performance at length. All he said was, "It's the same as before."

The next night, against Washington State, Bob was in the starting lineup. With thirty-eight seconds to play, Cal led 80–76. Bob rebounded a teammate's missed free throw, was fouled, and made both of his free throws to ice the game. Then with only one second remaining, Critchfield threw a long pass to Bob, who took the ball under the bucket and stuffed it. The Harmon Gym crowd of five thousand rose to applaud this illegal, irrelevant gesture. Bob smiled and walked into the locker room.

The next weekend Cal lost in the Northwest to the two Washington teams. Critchfield didn't shoot well; Presley had foul problems and continued raging at the refs. Only loose and easy Gaines played with consistency. Then Cal won three in a row; in the third game, against Southern Cal, Critchfield blazed in overtime, and Bob, tough in the stretch despite taunts about his haircut from the L.A. Sports Arena crowd, finished with thirty-one points. He was in good shape emotionally, it seemed, for the game the next night against UCLA and Alcindor.

The second confrontation was worse than the pre-strike game. Alcindor completely obliterated Presley, scoring thirty-two points, grabbing twenty-two rebounds, blocking seven shots. Bob did manage twenty points, but they were meaningless. UCLA won 115–71.

Cal's season ended early in March with home-and-home games against Stanford, winning at Harmon and losing the next day. In the finale, Critchfield scored seventeen points, enough to break the all-time Cal conference scoring record. Presley had only nine points, plus a horrendous two-and-one-half-minute stretch early in the second half: the Bears were coming back from a big deficit when Bob suddenly followed in a teammate's missed shot with an illegal stuff, goaltended a Stanford shot, then again jammed an impermissible shot of his own. These indiscretions turned the tide toward Stanford. Cal lost 64–51 and finished the season at sixteen and nine and fourth in the conference, the only time a Herrerias team reached the first division of the Pacific-8.

More notable that afternoon was the performance of the California freshman team. Jackie Ridgle hit for twenty-one points, a bit below his thirty-point season's average, for a frosh team that finished seventeen and one. A tribute, some said, to Padgett's recruiting and coaching work with the freshmen.

Herrerias had one year left on his contract at Cal. "I'm still happy with my job," he said after the Stanford game. "I'm not contemplating leaving Cal."

Newell said he wasn't contemplating changing coaches. He denied rumors Rene's job was in jeopardy. The only person who could fire Herrerias, he said, was Herrerias himself. Three days later, on March 12, Newell resigned, to be effective at the end of the semester. Then on April 11, so did Herrerias.

The Presley case was neither the only straw nor the last straw for Pete Newell. He said he had been ready to leave Cal months earlier but wanted to make sure the

football program was in sound shape. Newell didn't like
the mood in Berkeley, the way things were going. "The
politics of the day don't meet things head-on," he said.
"They just defuse them. And you can't operate that way
in sports, not when you have to play a game every few
days. The climate in Berkeley is very bad."

Newell thought that Presley "was put in front to lead
a cause he probably didn't subscribe to, and it became a
heady thing for him." And Herrerias? "He was caught
in the climate," said his mentor, "a victim of it."

Newell was perturbed by what he considered admin-
istrative concessions. He felt the chancellor's office was
capitulating to the dissidents. Whenever he spoke to
alumni groups, he was asked pointed questions about
campus policies. He had the answers but couldn't con-
done them. "As time went along, it got harder to sell our
athletic program to conservative alumni," he said. When
he could no longer defend his bosses, he quit.

Coaching had been more satisfying to Newell; a coach
had direct control over his destiny, at least in the old
days. But these new, complex times were befuddling to
a man everyone viewed as soft-hearted. "The racial implications surprised me," said Newell. "It's sort of an
indictment of athletics. I always felt that athletics were
above social problems, but athletics have allowed society's ills to catch up."

He hoped the chancellor's fact-finding commission
might be supportive—but the hope was hollow. They
tended to come down on the side of the black athletes:
more tutoring, better summer jobs, more consistent
financial aid. Newell got the message, and so, soon, did
Herrerias.

"Rene and his wife sat down to discuss the alterna-

tives," said Newell. "He realized that when you're
painted with a smearing brush, it takes a long time to get
that paint off of you. I felt it would be best for Rene to
leave. If he'd stayed, he couldn't have accomplished anything because there'd been so many prejudgments made
against him. And the administration seemed to think
that if Rene left, it would make things easier for them;
it would resolve their problems."

Rene left, embattled and embittered, "in the best
interests of my family and myself. I feel I am leaving
the basketball program on sound footing." He recommended that Padgett "receive strong consideration" for
the head coach's job.

(Herrerias never coached on the college level again.
Nearly a decade after his experience at Berkeley, he still
refused to discuss the Presley case. "It's the kind of
thing I just never want to think about or talk about," he
said. "Please try to understand." Through the years,
when Herrerias met with old friends, he never said anything disparaging about Presley. There was a reunion
of Cal basketball alumni early in the summer of 1975,
not long after Presley's death. During cocktails one man
joked, "Well, Rene finally got rid of Presley." Ned Averbuck winced when he heard the comment. "A few people
sort of laughed to be polite," Averbuck said, "but not
Rene. I looked over to where he was sitting, and he'd
put his head on the table and said nothing.")

Averbuck was one of Padgett's leading boosters for
the head coaching job. Two days after Herrerias's resig-
nation, Averbuck, Newell, and sports information director Bob Steiner met at Newell's house to talk about
Rene's successor. Averbuck argued that Padgett might go
elsewhere if he weren't promoted at Cal. "Padgett's
already told me he's starting to look around," Averbuck

said. Steiner feared that Padgett lacked proven big-college coaching credentials, yet he also believed Padgett was the only man for the Cal job at that moment.

Averbuck sensed that Newell had reservations about Padgett's coaching ability. Newell had hired Padgett as a recruiter, not a coach. But Newell ended up agreeing that Padgett was the best choice to coach the players Padgett himself had recruited. As a backup, Newell brought in as assistant coach a man the black athletes had asked for—not by name, but by color: Earl Robinson, who'd played for Newell on Cal's 1957 NCAA championship team and had briefly been in major league baseball.

Cal's returning players were ecstatic about their new coaches. "This is just great," Presley enthused. "Now I'm looking forward to playing."

Gaines thought there'd be no hangover of the tensions of the previous season. "All of the players, whites and blacks, are delighted coach Padgett got the job. We're looking forward to a great season."

Robinson hoped he could "lend some insight to some of the problems. It's a great opportunity. I've always been interested in helping young people receive their education and make their transition to the community."

Padgett didn't expect any trouble from his players, nor did he feel that his close friendship with his players would diminish team discipline. "Discipline comes from within. I've always been fortunate to work with players who respect what I've tried to do. They've always conducted themselves well, and I don't anticipate any problem here."

Bob moved out of Gaines's place and into an apartment of his own, on Parker Street, in late spring 1968.

There weren't many things to move, just clothes and his
record albums: Miles Davis, Theolonius Monk, Cannon-
ball Adderley, Horace Silver, Roland Kirk, and Bob's
favorite, Charlie Parker. He bought a hot plate, and
Adriana got him a table lamp and a bedspread for the
large, furnished room. Rent was cheap enough, only
fifty dollars a month, and now that he had a pleasant
summer job teaching ball to kids at a Berkeley recreation center, Bob always had a few extra bucks. He continued to take handouts from Sylvia and now persistently asked Adriana to work on the street for him, but
she just as persistently refused. Early in the summer she
went to visit her family in Virginia, where Bob phoned
her frequently. The Wheelers knew about her relationship with Presley and tried to persuade her to break up
with him.

"That summer was turmoil," she remembered. "Bob
calling all the time. My parents telling me to tell him
not to call. Him still calling. Around and around. By
the time the summer was over, I'd convinced myself to
break up with him."

Bob spent much of the early summer in the company
of teammate Waddell Blackwell, who also had relatives
in Detroit. He was a loner and saw the same quality in
Bob. He also dated whites. The two young men discovered they enjoyed cooking and took turns making dinner
for each other, laughing about their unmacho hobby,
realizing they'd learned by watching their mothers. Waddell was nearly a foot shorter than Bob and not as single-
minded about basketball. He was an excellent student,
on a scholarship in business administration. He had the
book smarts, Bob the street smarts. "You can read people," Waddell told him, "but I'm not sure you know
what to do about it." And Bob wasn't sure himself.

A man who was leaving the neighborhood gave Bob a Doberman. Bob called the dog Slim and eventually gave the same nickname to Sylvia, Adriana, and other women. He never went anywhere without Slim. The dog was good company with Adriana away, and Bob admitted to himself that as much as he thought he wanted to be alone, it was still necessary to have someone around, even a dog.

A friend of Bob's told him, "You're affectionate only with dogs. The only things you get along with are dogs and kids."

"Dogs don't make demands," Bob answered. "Dogs give and never take. You can trust your dog. If you trust people, they let you down. Dogs don't let you down."

Bob dropped by the athletic department frequently during the summer. Padgett always had time to chat; he was extremely optimistic about the coming season, and from the way the coach talked, Bob was sure all his problems on the court were solved: no more hassles with a head coach.

"That man," Bob observed, "is so sharp he could sell you a sewer."

Late in August Bob noticed a new secretary in the athletic department, tall, and apparently very confident. One of the older secretaries told him the new girl's name was Rae Oreskovic. Within a month he was seeing her regularly.

9

RAELENE MARIE ORESKOVIC was nineteen years old, five-ten, and unhappy. She came to Berkeley early in 1968 because she was tired of partying, changing jobs, changing roommates. She was looking for something she'd never had: stability.

Rae was the only child of a career army officer and a housewife-mother, both with roots in Eastern Europe. The name Raelene was a combination of her father's first name, Raymond, and her mother's middle name, Helene. Raymond Oreskovic always made it clear he would have preferred a son. Earlier, the Oreskovics did have a boy, but he lived only a month.

"Your older brother would have been a great man if he'd lived," Rae's father frequently told her.

"You never wanted me," Rae always said. "You don't love me." And her father answered by beating her. He was a commanding presence: six-two, stocky, and strong; a man who easily gave orders but never, as Rae came to learn, took them. "He hated to be told what to do," she said.

He dictated Rae's every move. If she disobeyed, she expected to be beaten. If in school she got a grade as low as a C, she had to tell him, "No excuse, sir," and submit to a whipping. He once spanked her with a foot-long board drilled with holes—"so it'll move through the air faster," he told her. He used belts, tennis shoes, whatever was handy. She feared him but did not hate him, and her mother's attempts to intercede in the whippings were always unsuccessful. Rae built emotional barriers. She became surly and smart-alecky around almost everybody but her father. But the sharpness was never malicious. People simply thought she was amusing.

And eventually she demanded explanations from her father. If he told her to do something, or not to do something, and didn't give her a reason why, she'd disobey him, but she always knew the consequences.

Oreskovic's military career kept the family moving. Rae was born in Columbus, Indiana, then lived in North Carolina, Germany, and several California cities before her father eventually retired from the army to run a bowling alley in Monterey, California. His wife, Marion, was an excellent bowler and taught classes for him. Business was good; Rae was doing well in school, twice skipping grades; and for a short time there was stability.

Marion Oreskovic, at five-eight, had a veneer of strength that covered a chronic high blood pressure condition. Still, she was a workhorse around the house, cooking and cleaning and looking after the family. On New Year's Day of 1961, Marion woke early, cleaned the kitchen, did two loads of laundry, and then, at 9:00 A.M., died of a cerebral hemorrhage. Rae was thirteen years old.

Three months after Marion's death, Oreskovic and his daughter moved a half-hour inland to King City, an

American Graffiti town; again he operated a bowling alley. Rae went to King City High School during the day and worked at the lanes nearly every evening. She was already five-nine, weighed 160 pounds, and wore glasses. She knew she was not at all pretty but was still too young to be concerned, or to know how to dress to minimize her abundance. "I'd walk around in a plaid shirtwaist dress with a bunch of slips under it and this bulky wool sweater. Most of the time," she said with a laugh, "I looked like four trailers standing in a row."

As usual, her wit attracted friends. To the guys at King City High she was like a buddy. To the girls she was no threat. She spent the first summer in her new home running with the older high school crowd. Because of her size, she never had any trouble getting served in a bar. Or in some guy's car. The summer consisted of Scotch or vodka in the afternoons and bologna sandwiches on raisin bread to sober up before going to work in the evenings. It was a time of total rebellion—every adventure but sex—for Rae. She and her father were too busy to be depressed about Marion's death. Within six months he remarried. Rae had not met the woman; she didn't even know her father was dating. He came home one evening, told Rae to dress and pack for a weekend trip to Reno, and then casually mentioned his wedding plans.

"How can you do something like this so soon?"

"You need somebody," he told Rae. "Your mother died just at the time you really need somebody."

It was a California family: Oreskovic and his daughter, Addie and her daughter, all in a three-bedroom house. Addie threw away all of Rae's old clothes and put her on a diet. She gave her a new hairdo and new bearing. Rae lost twenty pounds. She liked Addie; she liked her stepsister; she liked King City. But this contentment lasted less than a year; Oreskovic had to keep moving on, this time up north a bit to Santa Clara.

Rae enrolled at her third different high school in sixteen months. Again, she sought out and was embraced by the fast crowd. They were more fun. Her father warned her never to hang around drive-in restaurants. She spent the summer of 1962 at drive-in restaurants.

Rae couldn't keep track of her father's jobs: bars, construction, weatherstripping, airline maintenance, insurance, electronics, laundromat, bowling. He had to manage, and if he was not permitted to operate his way, he'd move on. It was a blur to Rae.

Slowly, Oreskovic's new marriage started to crumble. Addie's daughter moved out within a few months, Addie herself within three years. Rae immediately put on more weight and tried to figure out ways to go off on her own.

Finally, late in 1964, when she was taking classes at San Jose State College and working as a salesperson in a men's store, she found a potential roommate, a twenty-six-year-old schoolteacher who'd been a neighbor of the Oreskovics in a Santa Clara apartment building. But the teacher was more interested in Oreskovic than in Rae, so the three of them found a larger apartment together. The teacher talked of marrying Oreskovic and was convinced otherwise by Rae.

"One night I came home and found my father sitting on his bed holding a forty-five in one hand and a Luger in the other. He'd lost control. He'd been drinking. He said he was going to kill me for ruining this romance," said Rae. But she was not frightened now, only very angry. She packed and moved, with the teacher, to another apartment in the same building. She was seventeen. She never lived with her father again.

Rae worked at a variety of jobs in the Santa Clara–San

Jose area for the next three years. Her weight ballooned
to 187 pounds. Occasionally Oreskovic harassed her
when he'd been drinking; she had to call the police.
But as time passed, their separation was total. She lost
herself in work, as a bookkeeper and photoengraver and
part-time college student, and dropped 50 pounds. She
had two different women roommates, the second a peri-
patetic party girl she'd known at Wilcox High in Santa
Clara. And, finally, she lost her virginity—with the
brother of a girlfriend, the first man who took a physical
interest in Rae. They dated for a year; then he left her
for another woman. Instantly she went on a sexual binge.
"The bag boy at the supermarket. Anybody," she said.

After that she worked out her physical frustrations
by ice skating. She discovered Berkeley's Iceland, and
Berkeley, and the UC campus. In February 1968, she
found a job as a secretary in the math department. That
summer she shifted to a higher-paying secretarial job in
the athletic department. She made $550 a month and
now could afford to live in a one-bedroom house. Alone.

(Her father also moved again in 1968. Oreskovic mar-
ried for the third time, went to Idaho, and, finally, to
Portland, Oregon. His third wife died there in 1974.
He continued to live, alone, in Portland.)

Bob showed up unannounced on Rae's doorstep early
one evening in late August. She'd never dated a black,
but she was no more unnerved by his color than by his
size (in platform heels she reached six-four).

Rae was nothing new for Bob; these affairs with
white women had predictable patterns. He had found
a new game.

"What kinda ladies you attracted to?" Rae asked.

He smiled at her bluntness. "Ladies who give me

things," he answered. "Money, jewelry, watches. I like ladies who buy things for me."

Rae covered her surprise. "I'm not into that trip," she said. But within a few months she gave him a few dollars whenever he'd ask, or, if she had extra money, even if he didn't ask. As time went along in their relationship, Rae felt that Bob needed her. She had a dependent, someone to take care of, and this was Bob's principal pull for Rae. For the first time in her life, she felt truly wanted, and this gave her, also for the first time, a sense of self-importance. So she stuck around.

Adriana returned to campus in September. She did not yet know about Rae but hoped Bob had found at least one Rae in her absence. Adriana wanted to break off with Bob. She was afraid to continue seeing him, not because of the beatings—which were an accepted part of the relationship—but because she feared Bob was too serious about her. She lost herself in details of sorority rushing in the early fall weeks and avoided contact with him, although he called frequently. She eventually went to Parker Street for a visit, and he kept her in his room for three days. He talked prostitution again. To shut him up, Adriana agreed to take a look at the requirements of the job. Bob borrowed a car and drove her to a corner on Fourteenth Street in West Oakland. "This is ridiculous," she said. She was very curious, though, and decided to stand on the corner and see what happened. "But don't drive off and leave me," she warned.

Within a few minutes two men approached her. Adriana caught a glimpse of grimy fingernails and immediately ran to the car and had Bob take her home.

"This is too disgusting," she told him. "Don't lay this on me anymore." Bob laughed. "Maybe you're just *too* white for this work, Slim." He never raised the subject with her again. Now he spoke more of marriage.

Adriana spent most nights at Parker Street. He cooked dinner; they made love; there were intermittent beatings. She couldn't bring herself to break it off and often considered becoming Mrs. Bob Presley.

"It could make things more stable," she said. "If you get in the pros and get a good contract, at least there'll be money and we can stop washing dishes in the bathtub." Adriana rationalized that mixed marriages were common among professional athletes. Why couldn't their marriage work?

But she merely mused—and then fretted about what her parents would say. She had not told them she was seeing Bob again. How could they ever accept her marrying him?

Bob begged her. He cried. He said he had tried to kill himself when she wouldn't accept his phone calls that summer in Virginia. He showed her scars on his wrists. But Adriana thought he was jiving her. Not until she met Rae did she learn that Bob indeed had taken a blunt knife to his wrists one evening in August in Rae's home. When the two women finally did meet, they became good friends. They had a lot in common.

Bob's life overflowed with people late in 1968. Evenings were filled with Rae and Adriana, overnights with Adriana, days—when the other two were working or in class—with Sylvia, who never seemed to have trouble eluding work for a few hours. Bob particularly enjoyed bundling with Sylvia just before practice or a few hours before a game. The other players teased him. "You'll sap your strength," Gaines joked. But Bob said nobody ever told him he couldn't, or that it was harmful.

When he wasn't with a woman, he was running with Waddell Blackwell or the first white male friend he'd ever had, a young man from Brooklyn named Don Geisinger. They'd met in a social science class, got to talking basketball and jazz. They argued about records and the game and women, but never fought.

Geisinger learned quickly to adjust to Bob's moods and to read them. He was permitted into Bob's life because he make no effort to guide it. He always knew where he stood with Bob, too; if forced to admit it, Don said he was a crutch, a friendly crutch.

"He just needs you or somebody else around him all the time for support and encouragement," a woman friend told Geisinger.

"Maybe so, but you've gotta stand by him because he just doesn't know how to do things," replied Geisinger. "And he's such an open guy, you gotta like him."

Geisinger had never known anyone like Bob. He considered him special. He told Presley, "You're not geared to be an average person. And I don't mean because of your height. Even if you had average height, you wouldn't have an average life. You're just in such a hurry."

And Bob was. He was in a hurry for Padgett to put together a team good enough to contest UCLA for the conference championship. He was in a hurry to become the Critchfield of this new season, the key man on the team, the big pointmaker, the leader, the locus of publicity, the player the pro teams would consider among their first-round draft choices in early 1969, the eventual recipient of a bundle of bonus dollars now that the two professional leagues, the National Basketball Association and American Basketball Association, were in a bidding war. He felt he was rushing toward a big financial finish and the moments along the way would take care of themselves. Padgett continued to assure him that everything would be wonderful; everything would be wonderful for everyone.

Earl Robinson, Padgett's black assistant, thought he'd been hired to coach, not serve as a team psychologist, "not to pacify black problems. But that's the only thing Padgett wanted from me," he said. "Mainly I was there just as an image for Padgett—to make him look liberal."

Robinson was always bitter about the 1968–69 Cal basketball season and about Padgett. "He used me, he used Presley, he used everybody," Robinson explained. "Anything to get himself more attention."

But not long before that season began, Bob himself was full of praise for Padgett. "The team has unity this year," he said. "The way we feel toward each other is one hundred percent better than last year, so there's no reason we can't be a better team. There's a different atmosphere. People are on my side now. They have faith in me. I feel important. We're all working hard to win, for ourselves and for Jim Padgett."

Presley felt that Padgett's preseason training methods had the team in fine physical condition. "Padgett is placing all the guys in a position of responsibility," he said. "We're learning for ourselves."

Sports Illustrated ranked Cal fifteenth in the nation in a preseason poll. Nick Peters predicted the team could finish with a record of nineteen and six. And on the eve of the December 2 opener against the University of San Francisco, Padgett suggested he had so many able players he was not certain, except for Presley and Jackie Ridgle, who would be in the starting lineup. He also admitted, "I feel the natural athlete can do more by accident than he can be taught. I've always said the secret to my success is having topnotch players. Our material is conducive to wide-open play. I hope all their natural talent will compensate for a lack of defensive ability at first. But if people don't like the way we play, I could care less."

Nick Peters was reminded of something Padgett had once told him: "I can't coach, that's why I go out and try to get the best players available." Peters had the impression Padgett was only half kidding.

The coach had continued to recruit the best players available. One of his plums in 1968 was a black superstar from Cal's backyard, Phil Chenier of Berkeley High. He chose Cal over champion UCLA mainly because of Padgett.

Gene Chenier, his father, a shipping clerk and a leader in organized youth sports in Berkeley, was very impressed with Padgett. "Jim became a good friend and took a personal interest," he said. "We got the impression that Jim would still keep coming around even if Phil went someplace else. Jim is concerned about Phil, and I'm sure he'll look after him. With Jim's reputation, a lot of good basketball players will be coming to Cal."

There was so much to anticipate for Cal basketball: a fine team with Presley and Ridgle this year, then in 1969–70 the likes of Chenier and returnees Gaines, Charles Johnson, Clarence Johnson, Blackwell, and Ridgle.

Padgett's packaging was unquestionably first-rate; his handling was estimable; a good rapport prevailed between coach and players. The only unresolved question was his ability to coach.

In the opener against San Francisco, Ridgle and Presley were superb, Gaines and Charles Johnson merely excellent as Cal won by eleven. The USF defense blanketed Bob all evening, but this sagging defense was overcome by Ridgle's thirty-five points. Ridgle was the new Rusty Critchfield. Bob had only thirteen points but played perhaps the best all-around game in his Cal career. He passed intelligently, rebounded consistently, blocked eight shots, forced the USF center to shoot from far beyond his range. It was a propitious night for such a worthy performance, for in the stands was Tom Nissalke, a scout for Milwaukee of the NBA. And Milwaukee desperately wanted to draft a good center the following spring.

There were four good college post men in the country that season, Nissalke noted, and he ticked off UCLA's Alcindor, Florida's Neal Walk, Houston's Ken Spain, and Bob Presley. "There's no doubt he'd be a first-round draft choice right now," Nissalke stated. "Everyone is looking for big centers who can block shots and get rebounds. One thing I like about Presley is his court posture. He doesn't get upset when things are going against him. The only negative mark he got was when he began slumping a little toward the end of the game. The only thing he needs is to knock some people around. You've got to be tough in the NBA."

Bob read the scout's comments and remarked, "If he wants to see me knock people around, he oughta come to a few practices." He laughed and added, "I'm on my way to the NBA."

The pro scout's praise buoyed Bob two nights later against San Jose State. He again played every minute and in this game scored thirty-five points and had fifteen rebounds as Cal won 103–98. And this time he didn't tire in the stretch: he scored seven straight points in the final 2:28 to break open a 94–92 Cal lead. "Bob proved again what I've been saying all along," boasted Padgett.

"He's one of the best players in the United States."

"First the NBA, now the U.S.A.," Bob told Rae, and giggled. "Maybe we're gonna win 'em all."

The San Jose game proved to Padgett that "when we get in trouble, I know we have to go to Presley. Bob's shown a lot of character to get where he has. It hasn't been easy, and it isn't a sure thing that it will get any easier. But he has great perseverance. The reason Bob's been successful is Bob."

Bob's confidence was shared by the team, and the Bears were so nonchalant three nights later against St. Mary's that it took a late hot streak by Ridgle to produce a seven-point Cal victory. Cal played poorly on defense; the mistakes of inexperience were obvious, although Bob had a decent game with eighteen points and fifteen rebounds. He was just as good in the next outing, against fourth-rated Cincinnati, which won by a point. Bob fouled out with seven minutes to play in a game Cal would have won had the team not taken so many foolish outside shots. The Cincinnati coach called Bob and Ridgle "two of the best players in the country," while Cincinnati center Jim Ard labeled Presley "one of the very best I've played against."

Cal split its next four games in out-of-state tournaments. Bob fouled out in the two tourney games in Portland, Oregon, where fans continued their booing of the previous year. Oregonians were not charmed by a player they considered a black militant, and there was constant speculation that some referees on the coast were less than equitable in their calls against Bob. The more calls against him, the more he fumed.

"The refs would let the other guys beat up on Bob in a game," protested Robinson. "And because Bob really didn't have a lot of years of experience, he didn't totally

understand that some of the physical play was a defensive ploy by the other team. So he'd lose his temper and
get more fouls. I guess maybe some white refs felt that
Bob was symbolic of the black revolt, and consciously,
or subconsciously, they let him get beat up."

Sometimes when a ref called a foul against a player
beating on Presley and awarded Bob free throws, Presley
would kneel down on the free throw line and mock a
broad display of gratitude to the official. Or he would
bow in supplication to the ref. Out-of-town crowds,
particularly in the Northwest, scorned his attitude.

"Bob must have been the most booed player in the
history of the Pac-8 Conference," commented Robinson.

California began its conference season on January 10,
1969, with an undistinguished five and three record.
The Bears lacked consistency and failed to find it during
the rest of the season.

"When we started to lose, everything fell apart," said
Jackie Ridgle. "I think we overrated ourselves. We
started getting tired in the second half of a game."

Charles Johnson concurred. The team was so over-
confident, agreed Presley, that "as soon as we lost a few,
we gave up."

Trent Gaines was more bitter than the others over the
early part of the season, and especially about Padgett.
"The man don't know a damn thing about coaching,"
Trent told Bob. Presley preached patience; Trent was
out of it, though. Gaines in fact walked off the team in
late January to participate in the Third World Liber-
ation Front strike on campus. The strike went on for
fifty-four days with an intermittent series of confronta-
tions and violent incidents as striking students demanded
an independent college for Third World studies.

Gaines tried to persuade Bob and Waddell to join the Third World walkout. He became the liaison between the strike leaders and some of the basketball players. Bob and Waddell were caught in the middle, and Bob turned to assistant coach Earl Robinson for advice.

"I could see Presley was torn by this thing," said Robinson. "He didn't know what to do. I told him to do whatever would make him comfortable. But I knew that Bob always did whatever he wanted to do."

A few days before the strike began, several fellow black athletes told Waddell and Bob, "We have to stick together. This thing won't work unless we're all in it together. We've got to show solidarity."

"We'll get back to you," replied Presley.

He saw that this turmoil was bigger than his "haircut" crisis of a season earlier. He knew that one more display of militancy on his part would completely wreck his prospects to be a pro. He would be in the scouts' books as a double troublemaker who hassled two different coaches in two years.

"It just ain't a good time to be black," he said at Blackwell's place the night before the strike.

"Doesn't look good either way," agreed Waddell.

He knew that Bob was an asset to the strikers: a figure of size and visibility, a crucial addition to the walkout. Waddell also knew how important basketball was to Bob.

"It depends where you're coming from," Waddell observed. "Maybe it depends on what you want later, and a little bit on where you've been."

Blackwell had come from a racially mixed high school. As had Charles Johnson. They were not swept up in the fervor of this racial strike. The pressure to participate was not as heavy on them either because they did not have the "star" quality of a Presley or a Jackie Ridgle.

Ridgle hesitated about joining the strikers. Like Presley, Jackie was at Cal for ball: Jackie wanted a pro
career; Cal was taking care of Jackie. Even when somebody put sugar in the gas tank of Jackie's car, Ridgle was
not intimidated. Ridgle did not strike. Nor did Charles
Johnson.

"We got to think of other things right now," Waddell
told Bob. "We got to think ahead still. I'm just really
confused. Whatever I decide, don't let me influence
you."

Presley opened a bottle of Boone's Farm blackberry
wine. He hoped that Waddell could convince him one
way or the other. He respected Waddell's mind. He
thought he could rely on Waddell to make the right
decision in a crisis.

"Makes sense for the blacks to stick together," Bob
said. "Makes sense to think about ourselves, too. About
our own lives and careers. I know that most of the
football players are behind the strike. But it's just like
last year—the football players got more to bitch about.
So we got to think like basketball players. We got to
think like individuals."

They talked most of the night without reaching a
decision, and the strike started the next day without
their participation. But they knew that by avoiding a
decision they'd actually shown that they didn't want to
join the strikers.

Forty-eight hours into the walkout, Gaines approached
Presley and Blackwell while the two were heading for
a class in Dwinelle Hall.

"Some of the brothers are pretty hot that you guys
haven't announced you're quittin' the team," Trent

warned. "You gotta be with us on this thing. Some of the brothers are talkin' trouble if you don't get involved. They say it could be rough for you."

"Hey, c'mon, man," Presley said, "you ain't makin' a threat here, are you?"

"I'm not makin' anything," insisted Trent. "I'm just passin' on what some of the brothers are sayin'. And they're sayin' you got to be with us right away." Gaines walked off without further comment. He'd carried the message.

"What you think?" asked Bob.

"Sounded hostile is what I think," answered Waddell. "I heard that Jackie got himself a shotgun. And maybe we oughta get ourselves a little protection, too."

Blackwell was frightened. He read Gaines's message as a threat—not from Trent personally, but from the strike leadership. They were looking to intimidate him. Blackwell didn't think Bob could be intimidated, but he wasn't sure. He figured nobody would mess with Presley one-on-one, especially because most of the guys knew that Bob had a ferocious temper. Waddell wondered if they were trying to get to Bob through him. Whatever they were trying to do, Waddell decided it sure couldn't hurt to get a gun. He had a friend who would lend him a pistol, and he picked it up late that afternoon.

He phoned Bob. "I got company for us," he said. "I'm gonna start packing it right now, and you and me and it are gonna stay together for a while."

"You're not afraid to pull the trigger if you have to, are you?" asked Bob.

"I'm not sure," Waddell admitted. "Guess I won't be sure until I have to."

"Well if you think you will be, just give it to me and I'll carry it. You just lemme know."

Cal had a basketball game that evening in Harmon Gym against Loyola, Los Angeles. There were indications that several of the Third World strikers would be picketing outside the gym, both as part of their overall protest and to harass the nonstriking black basketball players. Presley and Blackwell walked to the gym together. The evening was mild, but Waddell wore a trench coat so he'd have a large enough pocket in which to carry his pistol.

They turned off Bancroft onto the dead-end street that led to Harmon. Bob asked, "How bad you think it's gonna be in there tonight?"

"Awww, Loyola ain't within fifteen points of us." Waddell laughed.

"I refuse to be amused," retorted Presley. "I ain't talkin' ball. You know that."

"We'll see in a minute," said Waddell. "It's at least gonna be a little hostile."

"You think it's too late to reconsider? Maybe we just shouldn't show up for the game. What do you think?" asked Bob.

Waddell continued to walk. "What do *you* think?" he countered.

"I think the die has been cast," stated Bob. "I think they know they can't push us."

They were surprised that there were only a handful of pickets outside Harmon. They thought maybe they'd overreacted. But as they were dressing in the locker room, another player warned, "The brothers are waitin' for us in the gym."

"Gee," said Bob, "our own cheering section." The dressing room was silent until the players went on the floor for the pregame practice.

As soon as they were visible to the people in the stands, Presley and Blackwell and the other black players were booed mercilessly. Several dozen blacks were clustered together in one area of the stands. Eggs came down on the floor. Each black player was cursed by name.

Blackwell was frightened. He didn't know what might be thrown down on him next. He practiced free throws and didn't make one. When he left the line, he stood next to Bob under the hoop for rebounds. They didn't speak. The noise from the stands was insufferable. They couldn't wait to get off the floor and into the locker room for the final pregame instructions.

Padgett had very little to say to his players. "Try to ignore everything but the game," he advised.

"It's OK," Earl Robinson told Waddell. "Just try to be cool out there. Just try to look cool if nothing else."

The tumult continued through most of the game. At halftime nobody said a word in the Cal locker room. During a time-out in the second half, Presley was on the verge of losing his temper. He walked over to Waddell on the bench and asked, "Why don't they just let us play?"

"I'd be happy," answered Waddell, "if they just let us live." He laughed halfheartedly, but he got Presley to smile a bit.

After the game, which Cal won, they walked to Blackwell's together. They had survived this storm and figured the worst was over. There were no more threats during the strike. The taunting was reduced to glacial stares when Bob or Waddell walked on campus with their white women.

The rest of the basketball season, however, was empty for Bob, except for the second UCLA game. The strike, and the team's lack of success, had dissipated his enthusiasm. There was nothing to look forward to—except that one last meeting with the Bruins and Big Lew. Their first meeting of that season had come soon after the beginning of the Third World walkout. It was in L.A., so the hostility was minimized, but Bob had been humiliated by Alcindor—outscored thirty-two to one— and UCLA had won 109–74. The final Alcindor-Presley meeting was another matter.

UCLA came to Harmon on March 1 with a record of twenty-three victories and no defeats; Cal was only twelve and eleven. Padgett had been starting Bob and four sophomores: Ridgle, Charles Johnson, Bill Duwe, and Bobby White. That game Ridgle and "CJ," as Johnson was nicknamed, combined for fifty-three points against the Bruins, and White sank a free throw with fourteen seconds to play to send the game into overtime (albeit an overtime dominated by UCLA for an 84–77 victory). Bob had played well. He and Cal reserve center Paul Loveday permitted Alcindor only ten shots from the field; he finished with just seventeen points. Bob had only seven but more than compensated with his defense and rebounding.

"Presley probably played one of his better games," praised UCLA coach Wooden, "and this is the best any team has played against us in three years, including that game we lost to Houston."

Padgett looked at the performance as a harbinger of the Bears' abilities for the next year.

In the season finale, a loss in double overtime to Stanford, Bob had fifteen points and nineteen rebounds. Cal's record was twelve and thirteen. Bob's average of 16.2 points per game placed him twelfth on the all-time Bears scoring list—his numbers were good but not impressive.

Nick Peters wrote in the *Berkeley Gazette*:

Presley's statistical plunge and frequent spells of languid play are a mystery to many, but not to those who care to scratch the surface and discover the constant turmoil which hounds this youngster ever since his haircut earned national attention last season.

Bob is big, he's black, and his "natural" haircut is the antithesis of what the conservatives profess constitutes the clean-cut, all-American image. Pro athletes are not targets for such abuse, but Presley is a handy example for goons to vent their anger. Presley is the hate symbol that epitomizes what the liberal Berkeley campus represents to right-wingers. He has been booed up and down the coast, especially at such conservative, lily-white outposts as Corvallis, Eugene, and Pullman.

If all this didn't bother the sensitive youngster, why did he average 18.9 points and 14.5 rebounds for a coach he didn't agree with in the dissension-riddled 1967–68 season, whereas greatly improved team unity lowered his scoring and rebounding averages this year?

I'm certain Presley declined to side with the strikers and stick with Padgett, whom he respects, for one reason—a chance to finish his senior season and play pro ball. A less sensitive individual might have overcome many of the pressures, but Presley couldn't. . . .

Bob told his friends the year indeed had been a mess. He ultimately questioned Padgett's coaching abilities. He complained about Padgett to Gaines and to Ridgle, to Adriana and to Rae. He felt Padgett's offense should have been built around him, not Ridgle. And he thought Padgett could not develop the proper tactics in crucial moments of close games. Bob even stormed out of one late-season practice when Padgett told him to stop being so physical with his own teammates.

He told Adriana he was frustrated because he hadn't become the star he thought Padgett would make him. "And I really don't like ball that much anyway, you know."

"Bob wanted big status so he could make the pros," said Ridgle. "I remember him telling me early in the season, 'You're gonna get your points because you're good. But I need help.' I couldn't help him that much, though, 'cause Padgett had me going inside a lot, and all Bob was doing was clearing out for me so I could go deep. As time went along, I got the feeling Padgett thought he was doing Bob a favor by getting him into Cal and letting him play."

By the time Ridgle finished his career at Cal, he too was down on Padgett. He believed the coach had not prepared him adequately for the pros. (Ridgle did make it, briefly, into the NBA; Padgett's most successful products in pro ball, though, were Chenier and Charles Johnson.)

Padgett had his own assessment of his first season as head coach: "We haven't begun to get technical. Our main concern was to develop our personnel. . . . I've realized it's not in the cards to start four sophomores in this league and expect to do well."

His Cal teams never did do well. Nor did the teams at his next coaching venue, the University of Nevada at Reno. He could recruit and, usually, handle. But he could not win.

"I don't think Jim made a lot of promises to people," said Dave Maggard, the man who finally concluded— with Padgett's concurrence, he added—that the coach would be better off leaving Berkeley. "But I think the way Jim approached people, they expected more. It was just his style, his way of saying, 'Everything will be OK.' Jim's style didn't fit here. The alumni were saying that we had super talent in basketball but that we weren't getting any results from that talent. I thought we'd spent a lot of money on recruiting, and I had to wonder what was being accomplished with these recruits. When Jim was an assistant to Rene, his strength was his availability to the players. As an assistant, he was a soother. But when he became head coach, he didn't change his role."

Padgett retired from coaching in 1976 to become a retailer in Reno. He admitted, "People always said that I was a good person but not much of a coach. Well, that may be a fair assessment, and if it is, I'm glad that's the case. I thought it was necessary to be close to my players. I wanted to contribute to their personal success. I did the best I could for Bob Presley at Cal."

Presley's future was up to Presley. With the season gone and the pro draft nearing, Bob could smell the money. No matter that he lacked sufficient credits to get a degree from Cal. The only degree he wanted now was a Bachelor of Bucks. The pros wanted good centers. And good centers made big money. He was at the point of not caring about technique or teamwork or titles. Basketball held interest for him not as a game, but as a bank. He told Adriana that only the money mattered. He could do better financially with a team in the two-year-old American Basketball Association because "I can grow with a newer team and become its top-paid player." But both leagues were tossing around big money, and he lusted for a bidding war over him.

In spring 1969, the Milwaukee Bucks of the NBA made UCLA's Alcindor their first draft choice. They'd pay him $125,000 a year. Among the other first-round draftees in the older league were Neal Walk, who got a remarkable $250,000 from Phoenix, and UCLA's Lucius Allen, paid only $35,000 by Seattle. The cream of the NBA first-round draft crop also included Jo Jo White, Herman Gilliam, and Butch Beard. The 143rd name on the NBA draft list in 1969 was Bob Presley, taken by Milwaukee in the eleventh round. The older league reckoned Presley was headed for Denver of the ABA, which had drafted him earlier. The supposition was correct. Bob opted for Denver in late April. He assumed he could step right in as starting center and become the team's star, even though Denver was spending bigger money for six-nine "hardship" draftee Spencer Haywood, from the University of Detroit and Pershing High School. Haywood's first Denver contract was $50,000 per season for three years, plus an annuity of $300,000. Presley wanted $50,000 a year, but settled for $40,000 and a three-year contract.

"We feel Bob can step right in at center and make Denver a threat for the championship," said Denver Rockets president Bill Ringsby. "We consider him a fantastic player who is destined to become a superstar. I'm very impressed with Bob's attitude toward professional basketball."

Bob was very impressed with the $5,000 he received immediately after signing the contract. He quickly used some of it to make a down payment on a new forest green Cadillac, financed at $202 a month over thirty-six months. Easy monthly payments for a superstar. All he had to do now was go to Denver and play basketball. The last thing he felt like doing was going to Denver and playing basketball.

Bob wanted to take Adriana and Slim the Doberman with him to Denver in the new Cad for the contract signing in late April. But Slim vanished from Parker Street one morning. "Stolen," Bob said. "Damned whites around here on my case stole him." Rae found a Great Dane pup for him. Another Slim. The pup was too small to travel, and Adriana didn't want to go.

"It's only for a day or two," she consoled him. "You

can handle it alone. And I've got too much studying backed up here."

"Just help me check out the town, that's all," he pleaded. "Maybe you'll like it there. Maybe you'll wanna move there with me in August. Can't hurt to take a quick look."

"We'll see about August when August comes," she replied. Adriana was ready to break completely with Bob. A perfect time with him moving on, and she had other plans for the summer.

So he went to Denver without a woman, quickly returned to Berkeley, packed, arranged for Adriana to take most of his final exams, and bought a plane ticket to Sweden.

"Black guys can have a good time there, I hear," he told Rae.

And he did. He tripped around Scandinavia for nearly six weeks and came back to Berkeley with three custom-made suits and a ring for Rae—pearls set in gold, platinum, and diamonds.

"He gave it to me one night after he beat the shit out of me," Rae said.

Bob sensed the split with Adriana and was now reluctantly transferring his affections, and other emotions, to Rae. He thought he'd have a better chance of convincing Rae to join him in Denver—and he didn't want to go alone.

"It's tough enough leavin' Berkeley and all my friends," he told Waddell Blackwell. "I'd just like to have one person I know with me. One woman. Adriana, if she'll come."

"How come you can't just break that off?" asked Waddell. "You're both always aggravating each other. She bad-mouths you; you bad-mouth her. I don't understand why you've stayed together this long. Makes no sense."

Bob rationalized it as "good aggravation. I always feel I can depend on her. That's why I need her with me in Denver; to have somebody nearby I can trust."

"What you got to worry about in Denver?"

"Oh, the money and maybe makin' the team." Bob told Waddell that he wasn't sure he was good enough to play for the Rockets. He was not comforted by his friend's insistence that the Rockets wouldn't have drafted him or be paying him so much if they didn't think he could play center in the ABA.

"Somethin' can always go wrong," Bob said. "Especially for me."

Another friend, BSU leader Frank Jenkins, told Bob to stop brooding about Adriana. Bob had moved into a flat shared by Jenkins and Gaines when he returned from Sweden, and he stayed with them until it was time to move to Denver.

"If you worry about Adriana, you won't be able to play good," Jenkins warned. "So stop staring out the window half the night. You must think you're in love."

"Maybe I am," Bob said.

"Just be loose," Gaines cautioned. "It's gonna be cool for you in Denver. All you have to do is go up there and just sit on the bench and you'll get your money. You got it made, Awesome. Made like jade, don't be afraid."

Geisinger tried to analyze Bob's apprehension about turning pro. "You're afraid to fail," Don said, "but I have a hunch maybe you're afraid to succeed, too. Afraid you don't know what to do with success." Geisinger was concerned that some of Bob's other friends enjoyed helping Presley spend the balance of his Denver bonus money. There were coke and pot parties. Nothing heavy

—Bob never was a doper—but he relaxed at these affairs, and so if he could afford the relaxation, he didn't hesitate to spend the money. And by playing host, he was accepted by more people. Acceptance was an unspoken priority.

Bob and Geisinger jogged around Oakland's Lake Merritt in July 1969 on an almost daily basis. Bob had put on a great deal of weight since the end of Cal's season in March; he'd promised the Rockets he'd lose it by August. He had dropped a few pounds, but not enough.

Geisinger considered Bob in decent enough shape physically. But psychologically, no. Geisinger could tell that Bob had no interest in Denver, or ball.

"Trouble is, I'm not qualified for anything else," Bob said. "What the hell else can I do? I'm trapped in ball, and I'm not good enough. Damned Padgett didn't get me ready enough."

"You'll be OK," Geisinger assured him. "You'll make it. You'll succeed. It'll be all right; you'll see." Geisinger wanted his friend to succeed, but he felt all along that "success wasn't in the cards for him." For weeks Bob vacillated about going to Denver. He worried aloud constantly. "I'll be OK if they don't hassle me about my first Berkeley season," he told Ridgle. "But somebody up there probably will, 'cause that's my luck. With my luck, I may never make it."

Geisinger and Blackwell kept at Bob to go to Denver. If he didn't go, there was the matter of refunding money he no longer had. There was his future to consider. And there was that forty thousand a year—in regular paychecks—just waiting for him.

Adriana moved to Los Angeles in early summer. Bob flooded her with telegrams and phone calls, pleading

with her to join him. But she was taken with another
man by now. A white man. "It's easier being with him,"
she said. "He's the first good relationship I've ever had.
He's rich and good-looking. There *are* other guys out
here in the world, you know." And she told Bob, flatly,
that she had no intention of ever becoming Mrs. Presley.

Bob flew to L.A. and went directly to Adriana's apartment. Her new friend answered the door. Bob told him,
with immense courtesy, to leave, and the man did. Bob
tied Adriana to a chair, grabbed a kitchen knife, carved
his initials just above her navel, told her how sorry he
was, left the apartment, and caught a plane back to
Oakland. When Adriana's friend returned, he wanted to
call the police, but Adriana told him to leave things
alone. She was sure that, finally, her involvement with
Bob had ended.

Bob was able to persuade Rae to come to Denver with
him for a few days. "I saw a clothing store there that
maybe I can buy and you can run," he told her. They
checked the place, but the prospects seemed too imprac-
tical to Rae, and she returned to her job as secretary in
the Cal athletic department. Bob was now alone in Denver; he'd even left the pup at Rae's.

Bob was in the hands of a black coach for the first
time. He had trained under Will Robinson at Pershing
High but had never played for him. Now he could finally
see how a black ran a basketball team.

The Denver coach was John McLendon, the first black
ever to preside over any professional team when he
coached Cleveland in the ill-starred American Basketball League. McLendon had been a fine coach on the
college—black college—level at Cleveland State, Ten-
nessee State, Kentucky State, and North Carolina Cen-

tral. The club he inherited at Denver this year had only one proven shooter, Larry Jones; one reasonably good big man, Byron Beck; and two promising youngsters, Haywood and Presley.

Haywood had spent thirteen thousand dollars of his up-front money to buy and customize a car. He poured thousands more into new clothes, a wardrobe of custom-made suits that put to shame the few garments Bob had bought in Sweden.

Bob refused to be intimidated by Haywood's splendor, and on the second day of preseason training camp he hired a limousine and a black chauffeur to drive him to the Regis College gym and wait outside until practice concluded. "I wondered if Presley had a full-time chauffeur," said Beck.

McLendon wondered only if Bob was in good condition.

"I'll give you a hundred and ten percent," Bob promised.

"Just so your hundred ten is the same as my idea of a hundred ten," said McLendon.

McLendon had never seen Presley play; Bob was drafted and signed before the new coach was hired. "The scouting reports on him looked good," acknowledged McLendon, "but if I had a choice after seeing him, I wouldn't have signed him. And I don't mean just because of the poor shape he was in. He had a funny shot: the ball wasn't in his hands very good when he shot. He couldn't give the ball any direction. All he had was a flat, turnaround jumper." And McLendon sensed other liabilities in his supposed new center. "He seemed so unsure of himself. He was nervous. He seemed disturbed about something, and I was never certain what it was."

"He gave off an air of maybe having personal problems," said Beck, "although some of the time he seemed pretty confident of himself. He had flashes of good execution—I frankly thought he had a lot of talent. But he just didn't produce consistently."

Larry Jones wondered if Presley could make the team. Jones had reason to question the hiring of a player like Presley; Larry, consistently one of the top scorers in the ABA, was making only $23,000, while unproven people like Haywood and Presley were starting off at much higher figures.

But Haywood had come to camp in shape, and to play for McLendon it was necessary to be fit immediately. McLendon demanded conditioning; part of his camp regimen involved running a mile a day in less than six minutes. He wanted a fast-break offense, and if a player wasn't in top shape, he couldn't run John McLendon's break. "I was trying to develop the Boston Celtics of the ABA," he explained. "My toughest workout is what I call X ray: a full-court, three-on-three game. X ray gives all my players a lot of opportunity to display their individual skills, but it gets them involved in team play, too. A workout like that 'X-rays' a player's skills, condition, and court sense."

"All things being equal," said Jones, "the players in the best condition would make McLendon's team. It was a very, very rough camp. Presley was big and burly enough to play pro, but he wasn't gung ho like a lot of young players. No intensity. Even when he did hustle, he didn't *look* like he was hustling."

Within a few days Bob complained to McLendon and other team executives that the Rockets were late paying him an additional five thousand in bonus money he'd been promised. Even when he got the money, he said his overall contract was unfair, that he signed for too little, that he was mistreated in negotiations.

McLendon thought that perhaps the argument over money was just a cover for another anguish. "A black kid comes to a pro camp in 1969 wondering if there's a quota system. The kid feels he has to outdo only the other black players to make the team—and he worries about having to outdo his own kind. And there's another thing with a kid like Presley: so many people are banking on him to make it in the pros; it's very prestigious for *others*—friends, family, his high school and college coaches—for him to make it. And so a kid like Presley gets to camp and sees so many players at least as good as himself, and he begins to doubt his abilities. Unless he has a great ego, unless he can see no one but himself, he usually can't overcome these doubts."

McLendon saw doubt in Bob every time he was due to go on the floor for an X ray. And the coach surmised, "There's no way he can run my six-minute mile."

Bob had a no-cut contract. McLendon probably would have tried to trade him—the coach believed Presley could play in another system—but Bob cut himself. He checked out of the team's motel on September 23, put five thousand dollars in the glove compartment of his Caddy, and drove back to Berkeley. He never played a single minute in the American Basketball Association.

10

BOB SPREAD a variety of excuses among his friends in
Berkeley when he returned from Denver. It was a contract problem, he told most of them; he'd been screwed
by different people, or he was being taken, or things
were going on under the table, or people he couldn't
trust were trying to run his life. "If I'd stayed up there,
they woulda had me playin' for nothin'," he pouted to
Jackie Ridgle.

Loneliness was another excuse. It would have been
OK if Adriana had been there with him; or if only Rae
had been there.

Bob leveled only with Blackwell. "The workouts up
there were much tougher than I ever expected," he
admitted. "Guess I wasn't prepared."

It was clear to Blackwell, Geisinger, Rae, and a few
others that Bob was in a deep depression, so frustrated
with what he saw as a deliberate self-failure that he was
doing as much as he could as quickly as he could to
compound that fall. He spent his final five-thousand-

dollar payment from Denver on any familiar face on the Berkeley streets who asked him for a handout.

"Some people [stuck to] Bob's bread like flies to honey," said Geisinger. Street people, even a few ballplayers. Within weeks the five thousand was dissipated. All Bob had left to show for his Denver experience was the Cadillac, now a hostage of hefty monthly payments.

Despite his frequent boasts to friends that he would "take care of" his family if he ever hit it big, nothing went back to Detroit. Edna Presley did not see a penny of the Denver bonus. But she had seen the Caddy, and the contract, and the dog, for Bob was home briefly in the early summer of 1969.

The Presleys had moved to another neighborhood nearly a year earlier. Edna was ill, with a broken arm and then pneumonia, in 1968; she thought a "change of scenery would help, and it did some." The older daughters by now were married and had children and their own places. McLister popped in and out. The younger daughters were in school, or working, or both. And the youngest Presley child, Denise, was starting to roam the streets a bit too often to please Edna and Robert. Ultimately they were forced to house her three children.

The injury and illness kept Edna out of a job for nearly two years, but Robert was doing well enough at Ford to keep things financially stable. They did not ask their athlete son for money.

"I could tell by his attitude that he thought he was gonna make it with the pros," said Edna. "He sat down next to me and started reading his contract to me with his eyes all big. I tried to listen, but this big dog of his jumps up on me and I like to die of a heart attack right then."

More startling to Edna was Bob's report of his love

life in California. He told her about a white woman he loved, Adriana. "I'm thinkin' of havin' her fly out here to meet you tomorrow," he said.

Edna was angry with her son. "You done just what Mr. Gaddy told you never to do—get mixed up with white women," she scolded. "Why couldn't you find a black girl and fall in love? I suppose you probably got her stashed here in town someplace and were gonna surprise us with her." Edna wasn't aware that Bob was only pretending he was still with Adriana.

"If you're gonna make such a fuss about this woman I love, I'm not even gonna unpack," Bob shouted. "I'm just gonna get back in my car and drive back to California. All I want to do is what you and Daddy did: you fell in love, you got married, you had your babies, didn't you? Well, I'm gonna do the same thing."

"Sure," raged Edna, "but I bet I'll never see a black baby from you." Bob tore out of the house and drove away—cooling off for a few hours. When he returned, Robert was home from his shift, and Bob let his dad drive the Caddy around the block a couple of times—with the dog sitting between the two of them. Robert didn't know if he was more frightened by the size of the car or the dog.

Edna didn't know what to expect when they came back; Bob had put his suitcase in the trunk.

"Please c'mon in now and unpack," she pleaded. "I'd like to see your clothes." But he hedged and told her to come outside. He opened the trunk and then the suitcase and showed her some of the things he'd bought in Sweden.

Then they picked up their conversation—this time calmly—about Bob's girlfriend. "It really don't make no difference to me who you fall in love with," Edna explained. "The only reason I was mad was because you didn't do what Mr. Gaddy said. You let somebody get in your way when you were told not to. I just don't know why you couldn't find yourself a black girl."

"Black girls don't know how to treat you, Mama. I can't help it that I love who I love. This girl is what I want. And this is what I'm gonna do."

Edna had never heard such anger in her son's voice— not directed at her. "That was the only time—the *only* time—he ever talked back to me, said anything mean or harsh to me, in his whole life."

Bob left Detroit two days later and didn't return until 1974.

In the days just after the Denver failure, Bob spent the bulk of his time with Rae, Geisinger, and Blackwell. He felt he needed comforting. He didn't want to be around strangers or anybody else who would ask him questions. He didn't want to have to answer questions about what happened in Denver. He didn't want to answer questons about anything. Smoking dope was easier than talking. Listening to music with Geisinger was calming.

Bob liked this idea of dropping out; if only he could figure out how to live where nobody ever bothered him, where he could be alone but still have somebody reliable, somebody helpful, somebody considerate of his needs like Rae, Don, or Waddell always around. Just one of them at a time would be fine. But always at least one of them.

He considered the depth of his failure. He tried to understand if coming up empty in Denver meant that he was finished as a ballplayer forever. He wasn't sure how to assess the results of the brief Denver experience. He told himself he had not failed as a player because he had not been there long enough for his skills to be assessed in an actual pro game. The pros could never say that Bob Presley was an incompetent ABA player. They couldn't say that about a guy who had never *played* in the ABA.

"My abilities are not in question," he told Waddell. "The only thing they can really say about me that's true is that I couldn't handle the workouts, that I wasn't up to McLendon's system. But they can't say that I can't deal with another coach's system. That ain't been proved. Not yet. Nobody can say that Presley won't make it yet in the pros."

As usual, Waddell listened in silence. He knew Bob didn't want anyone else's interpretation of the Denver experience. The kindest thing—the only thing—he could do was just listen.

One evening in late September, Waddell excused himself from Bob's conversation. "Gotta date, man. You be OK here?"

"Uh, sure," Bob answered. "I'll be waitin' when you come back."

"Come along if you want to. We're just gonna have some wine on Telegraph or something."

"No, that's OK. Go ahead."

Five minutes after Waddell left, Bob called Rae. No answer. Maybe she was ice skating. Then he tried Geisinger. No answer. He phoned Iceland to see if Rae was there, but a girl told him she was too busy to page anybody.

Bob knew where Waddell kept the makings, so he rolled a joint, turned on the radio, and smoked for more than an hour while he listened to KJAZ, a little FM station out of Alameda that didn't assault the listener with too many commercials. He never understood how the damn station could stay in business with no business.

Lorez Alexandria was winding down on "Show Me," and Bob uncoiled himself from the couch and walked to the phone and tried Rae and Don again. Still no answer. He wondered what he could do until Waddell came back.

He was woozy from the dope. He thought about walking down to University to a pancake house but thought he might see somebody he knew, somebody he didn't want to see, somebody who would ask him about Denver.

A big band medley was on now. Basie. Herman. Somebody else. Bob phoned a bar on Telegraph, but the guy who answered said nobody named Waddell Blackwell was there. He thought about calling Detroit, but it was too late. He considered phoning McLendon in Denver to tell him he'd made a mistake, to tell him his life was a mistake ever since he was a kid in Detroit. He wanted to apologize to McLendon. To somebody. He needed somebody to talk to.

From the bathroom he could hear Charlie Mingus. That mean old Mingus, walkin' off if they didn't pay attention to his set. Fair enough. Screw 'em. Just walk right off and leave 'em with nothin'. They don't listen or pay attention, just get off.

He flushed and opened Waddell's medicine cabinet. Nothin' but toothpaste and aspirins and Sominex. Maybe take some Sominex and then sleep until Waddell came back. It would be easier to wait if he slept.

He dropped the jar, and it broke on the tile. He kicked it out of the bathroom, down the hall, and into the kitchen. He should have gone out with Waddell. He was mad he didn't. He was mad that Rae wasn't answering her phone, that Don wasn't at home, that it was too late to call Detroit and too stupid to call McLendon. He pulled out the silverware drawer and emptied it onto the small kitchen table. He screamed at the announcer on the radio to quit talking about who was playing at what nightclub in San Francisco and to start another record. He raged at the Sominex bottle for being broken. He slammed his fist against the handle of the refrigerator. He picked up a small steak knife and sliced first his left wrist and then his right. Ellington was now on the air, and Bob sat down on the kitchen floor to listen. There was no pain. He wasn't sure where the blood was coming from.

Bob was comatose when Waddell returned. Blackwell phoned Rae and Don and told them to come right over. He began bandaging Presley's wrists, and when Rae and Don arrived, they helped him finish.

Geisinger spotted the Sominex bottle. He assumed Presley had tried to OD on the sleeping pills. "Keep him awake. Gotta keep him awake."

Rae slapped his face. Blackwell gave him coffee. Geisinger washed him with a cold cloth. The radio kept playing. Nobody talked. Nobody asked any questions.

"If he wants to talk about it, fine," Geisinger said. "But he doesn't. So it doesn't seem right to ask him."

Bob recuperated at Geisinger's. He was glad they hadn't demanded any answers. If they had, he didn't know what he'd tell them. He was not sure if he had actually tried to kill himself. He remembered being very mad, but he didn't know what he'd been so mad about. Failing? And now he'd failed again. If he'd been serious about killing himself, he'd sure blown it. He couldn't even do a wrong thing right. But it had been easy trying. Quick and easy. That much he remembered.

Bob felt after a few days at Don's place that it was time to move along. He'd thought about how to pull

himself up. Money was his immediate crisis; he didn't
want to lose the Caddy, or pawn his new clothes.
"Wouldn't fit anybody else anyway," he said.

In early October, after conversations with a couple of
guys on the street, he decided to follow the ghetto status
course, and so he approached Rae with the same prostitution proposition that Adriana had rejected. He could
buy time, thinking time, if Rae kept him in money.
Meanwhile, something would come along; something
had to come along.

Rae let him speak his piece without interrupting.
She'd half expected him to ask. She was not insulted.
She was not angry. "What the hell," she said when he
finished talking. "Maybe it'll be amusing. Why the hell
not?"

Rae knew very well that Bob was using her, but it took
her years to figure out why. "Because I worked in the
athletic department for Padgett, I guess he saw this as a
way to get even with Padgett. And of course because I
was white he probably felt this was a way to get even
with all whites; this was his form of bigotry."

Rae was always aware that Bob felt more deeply about
Adriana than her. "She was his love, and I was his
sense," she said. And also adventurous enough to work
the street. Rae's spirit, her bent to poke around life's
cubbyholes, sent her to the streets as much as her affection
for Bob—and her fear that he might possibly beat her
senseless if she didn't do this work for him. He needed
money any way he could get it, and if she was making
enough as a secretary to meet his car payments, then she
would have helped him that way. But she wasn't, so she
took the second job.

One of the three brothers who controlled the vast
majority of hookers in Oakland agreed to break Rae in

on the same corner as one of his main ladies—on Seventh Street in the West Oakland ghetto. Rae's initial rates were, in the jargon, ten and two—ten for oral sex, two to screw. She used a room above a record shop. The first night's receipts were seventy dollars, but the amusement and initial excitement were soon translated into boredom—within hours. "It got really dull really fast," said Rae. So as not to interfere with her sleep and weekday job at the university, Rae worked the street only on Friday and Saturday nights and rarely past 12:30 A.M., "unless it got very busy."

When she was bored to the point of telling Bob, "I don't feel like it tonight," he'd threaten to beat her—so she managed to feel like it. After several weeks, Bob moved her to a spot where the johns could afford to spend more—on Grove Street—and arranged for her to use a hot sheet room just behind a large Sears, Roebuck department store. In that spot she was making as much as twenty dollars a trick. But the arrangement was brief. Bob had made the mistake of setting her up on a corner historically in the hands of a veteran black pimp, and Rae was cutting into his revenue. Late one night a shot was fired out of the window of a passing car, and Rae was grazed in the lower left arm. She was hospitalized for a couple of hours and then told Bob, "That's it. No more. Party's over."

"Take a day off," he pleaded. "We'll find another spot for you tomorrow night." But that next evening Rae drove to San Mateo and spent a week with a friend. When she returned to Berkeley, she told Bob she was definitely finished.

"OK," he relented, "you don't have to do what you were doing anymore. I got a better arrangement. One regular for a hundred bucks every time." And Rae agreed. She serviced only Bob's client and one other hundred-dollar-a-night fellow she found on her own. She split the take fifty-fifty with Bob in a career of prostitution that lasted only eight months. "I guess it was all that strong discipline I got from my father as a kid that kept me working the street. Being told you *have* to do something."

Rae maintained that her relationship with Bob was "like a gorilla living with daisies—but I'm not saying who was the gorilla and who represented the daisies."

Their fights, much as those Bob had with Adriana, were a case of mouth against fist. Both of the women were far brighter than Bob. They knew they had this advantage, and so did he. They knew they could use their quick, glib mouths to taunt him whenever they wished. They knew they could be acid. To them, sarcasm was a form of humor, and because Bob was slow, they often got away with taunting him. Talk was their equalizer. They knew when they went too far; they could tell when they had provoked him. But often they didn't care that their bad-mouthing forced Bob into the only reaction familiar to him: beating them.

"He beat me because he didn't know what else to do, how else to get back at me for something I did or said that he didn't like," said Rae. "He told me that's the way his father had handled his mother, and that usually his mother would fight back. He told me, 'They ended up in a draw most of the time. But you shoulda seen my mother. If you only knew how good black women really can fight.' Bob talked to me a lot about his folks fighting. I guess it was just something he accepted as normal, and I guess he saw nothing wrong with him behaving the same way. I came to understand that when a woman is smarter than a man, she beats him verbally and his only recourse is to beat her physically."

The beatings were confusing to Rae at the beginning of her relationship with Bob. Early on, she wasn't prepared to analyze either Bob's rages or the black-and-blue outcome of them. She finally decided that if she were going to continue to be a part of his life, she'd best try to understand his behavior.

She said, "I found a few psychology books, and what I read was that when a man felt insecure about his manhood, particularly a black man, the only way he knew how to react was by fighting. But the thing was that even after I read all this stuff and got to believe it, I still would provoke Bob into beating me. I guess because I knew the only other alternative was my not saying anything. And I just couldn't stand to come home to him and vegetate, to just sit around and not say anything about my life, about my work, about my feelings. I could never just be a lump. So, hell, if it meant provoking him into beating the shit out of me, that's what I had to face. I just accepted it, no matter how often it happened, and it probably happened on the average of once a month.

"Look, I had grown up in a house where I'd seen my mother beaten by my father. She took it, and she stayed. I took it, and I stayed. If you've never lived that way, if you've never grown up that way, it probably doesn't make any sense to you. You probably think a woman is crazy just to hang on and stay and keep taking it. It's just like if you never lived in Hong Kong, you wouldn't understand how it is to live in Hong Kong."

And so she always stayed. And the rationale, the conclusion she'd reach the morning after a beating when Bob was calm and apologetic and loving and begging for forgiveness, the conviction Rae always ended up with was that she stuck around because "I needed to be needed. He made me feel needed. He made me feel like a person—a loved person. I guess I let myself be beat because I loved him and I didn't want him to leave. I didn't want to lose him. Without him I would have been like a fire without wood."

Bob once signed up for a correspondence course in airline ticketing procedures. He was considering, he told Rae, trying to get a job with the airlines, starting at the bottom and maybe working his way up to a big money position in the front office of some airline.

When the course material arrived, he began reading the assignments, but he read very slowly. A particularly complicated chapter took him an entire day to read. Often he would have to reread a single paragraph over and over to comprehend its meaning. He had never learned how to read properly.

At the end of each chapter there were questions to be answered and mailed back to the correspondence school. By the time he reached the third chapter, he admitted to Rae that he needed her help.

"I've been readin' over these questions for the last two hours," he complained. "They just don't make any sense. Can you help me figure 'em out?"

He handed Rae the textbook. Within fifteen minutes she covered the material that had taken him more than a day to absorb. Then she looked at the questions and gave him all of the answers in another twenty minutes.

"That ain't fair," he protested. "You just skimmed that book. How come you can answer that stuff so fast?"

"If you don't like my answers, turkey, do it yourself," she said.

He doubled his right fist and popped her in the left eye and then walked out of the room. He never bothered with the correspondence course again.

Early in the fall of 1969, with the Denver washout almost fading from memory, Bob came to Rae with a new business proposal. This "deal" was more flippantly conceived than the pimping. It was a product of a dreamy cocaine-snorting session with a Telegraph Avenue street type named Bernard, who represented himself to Bob as a fine criminal mind.

Bob attempted to establish his own underworld credentials with Bernard. "My daddy was one of the great bootleggers in all of Alabama," he boasted. "And then in Detroit, too." Bob fictionalized Robert Presley's casual capers at the Alabama family still into sinister tales of interstate operations. Friends who overheard this storytelling had to restrain themselves from giggling. Gradually, Bob was working himself into a criminal frame of reference. If ball wasn't the answer, he suggested, why not the ghetto fallback: big-time crime.

Late in October Bernard told Bob of his foolproof plan for making a few grand in a short time. "Travelers' checks," Bernard said. "You buy 'em, then you lose 'em. But you don't really lose 'em. Dig?"

Bob had heard of travelers' checks but had never had reason to buy any. He did not, however, want to appear uninformed and searched for an explanation from Bernard without making it appear that he needed one. But all he could come up with was: "Who does what when?"

"OK," said Bernard. "You got girlfriends, right? Better to use chicks in this than yourself. Especially 'cause you're who you are. You got to stay behind the scenes." Bernard laid it all out.

On November 2, Bob came to Rae with the scenario. There was no way she would participate, she protested. He slapped her face: she would do this or he would hurt her more than he had in the past. "And there's some other folks in this with me who'll hurt you worse," he added. "You do it."

On November 3 Rae went to her bank, the Wells Fargo branch at College and Ashby in Berkeley, and bought $450 worth of American Express travelers' checks with cash Bob had given her. He sat in the Caddy parked in front of the bank and watched. He spent the evening with her and the next morning drove her back to the same bank, where she reported the travelers' checks as well as her checkbook missing. She filled out some forms and was given another batch of travelers' checks.

Rae was scared—of Bob, of the cops. But more of Bob. He stayed with her again that night and the next day. On the evening of the fifth, the two of them set out with Bernard for Los Angeles. They arrived in Beverly Hills in mid-morning, just in time for bank opening. Bob told Rae to start cashing travelers' checks: the ones she'd reported missing. She went to three banks and within an hour had converted the checks to $450 in cash.

"Now let's get you some presents," he said.

"I don't want a damn thing from you," she protested.

"You're going shopping," he ordered. A threat was implicit in his tone. Rae waited for him to give her some cash, but instead he handed over her checkbook. "Use these," he said. "And don't do your signature too good." Rae now understood that she was to buy herself presents by "forging" her own name on her own checks, the checks she'd reported missing at the same time she reported the disappearance of the travelers' checks.

Bob pulled in front of I. Magnin's and practically

shoved her out of the car. "Get somethin' you like a lot," he said. "We'll be waitin'." As Rae started to go inside, she saw the Magnin's doorman walk over to the Caddy and tell Bob to pull away. She heard Bob explain that he was "the lady's chauffeur."

Rae knew she had to come out of the store with merchandise that would please Bob—show him she was doing as he wished. She bought a two-hundred-dollar suede coat without any problem because she had identification to back up her own check. She had to concentrate, though, on signing her name. She almost forgot to make her signature look forged.

Rae handed Bob the box; he put it in the trunk and told her to help herself at other stores along the block. At J. Magnin's she picked up a pair of suede shoes and a pair of alligator shoes. Then, at another place, two dresses. Everything went into the trunk of the car. She'd spent at least five hundred dollars—and she never again saw any of the merchandise. When the shopping spree ended, Bob told her to start driving back to Berkeley. He and Bernard were tired.

On November 10, Bob visited an old campus girl-friend named Dina. She was to buy travelers' checks, he said. When she refused, he hit her. He gave her five hundred dollars, the bulk of which had come from the "replacement" travelers' checks Rae had cashed. He drove Dina to another Wells Fargo branch in Berkeley and went into the bank with her while she bought the checks. He took her back to her apartment and told her he'd pick her up the next morning and take her back to the bank so that she could report the travelers' checks stolen. Just as Rae had done, he said. After he left, Dina walked to the Berkeley Police Department and told an officer all the details. At nine thirty that night Bob stopped over to remind Dina about plans for the next morning. While he was at Dina's, she telephoned police. Officer Alan Pascoe came and arrested Bob, then drove to Rae's and arrested her. She was charged with grand theft, Bob with grand theft and soliciting to commit a crime: both were jailed. Within a few days they were freed on bond. Their preliminary hearing in Berkeley-Albany Municipal Court did not take place until January, and the trial itself was not concluded until midsummer of 1970, when Bob and Rae were living together as managers of a seventy-unit apartment building at Telegraph and Twenty-fifth in Oakland. They had pleaded guilty and were awaiting sentencing.

As part of the probation report on Bob, Alameda County deputy district attorney John J. Meehan told Superior Court Judge Harold B. Hove:

Defendant Presley is fairly well known in the Bay Area due to his having played center on the University of California basketball team a few years ago. It is felt no special consideration should be given to him merely because he participated in athletics at the university. The fact, however, that Presley did attend the University of California and was afforded the opportunity to have a higher education would seem to indicate a person of his caliber should have more awareness of his deliberate violations of the law. The scheme devised by Mr. Presley in making use of these girls to carry out his criminal conspiracy should be treated in the harshest manner. It is recommended that the defendant receive a commitment to the California State Prison.

Alameda County deputy probation officer Frank H. Robinson had several long interviews with Bob before submitting his own presentencing report to Judge Hove.

In one interview Bob told Robinson:

> Some people have a dream to be a big-time thief. They
> either lose this dream on their own or are forced to lose it
> by going to jail. I have lost my dream. Jails only make good
> people bitter and more hateful; they stop progress. I think
> if I go to jail it will be many years before I can progress. This
> is especially true since I now have a good opportunity with
> the job [building manager] I have. I would not want to lose
> this opportunity. I would like probation because I know I am
> not a thief. I committed a crime, but I was once what is known
> as a respectful member of society, and given a chance I will
> be one again.

Robinson also talked to Rae. "She shows a motherly
concern for the defendant," he told the judge. "She con-
tinues to voice nothing but praise for the defendant, not-
ing his strength and denying his faults. It appears that
both need and use each other for their own gains, although Presley has stated that if he ever married, it
would be to Miss Oreskovic."

Robinson recommended leniency. The probation officer implied that Bob, with Rae's emotional support,
would go straight.

Presley's lawyer was one of Alameda County's leading
black politicians, John George, a onetime track athlete
at Cal. "Bob thought this arrest had blown his whole
future life," said George.

"But your size is something you can cash in on," the
attorney told Presley.

"To most people I'm a freak," Bob answered. "Most
people don't see that I'm just a human being."

George contributed his notions to the probation report. He wrote, "Bob Presley was near famous because
of his basketball skills, but he did not want to be. Since
he was a near-famous person, people mistakenly think
that he leads some sort of glamorous life. Let me tell you

that he has led a life of loneliness. Bob Presley needs compassion and guidance at this time. He is a good candidate [for probation]. . . ."

Rae was a better candidate. On September 23 she was granted probation by Judge Hove, who warned, however, that if she continued to have any association with Bob, he would consider that contact a probation violation and jail Rae.

However, when Jim Lia, Rae's attorney, pleaded with the judge to permit the probation department to evaluate the possible dangers in the relationship, Judge Hove backed off. "I am not making any restrictions on marriage," he pointed out. "Presley helped you get into this mess, but then you are back and forth together again. You are in a mess, but you can't stay apart. If you are going to get together, well, marry him. Do it properly. But start making something of yourself."

Nothing could be done properly for several months. Hove had sentenced Bob to six months in Alameda County Jail. Bob ended up doing four months and twenty days at the prison farm in Santa Rita. His only visitors were Rae, Waddell Blackwell, and Don Geisinger.

During her visits Rae and Bob talked only in vague terms about the future. Both were broke. The Cadillac bought with his Denver bonus had been repossessed. Just before he started doing time, all they had to live on was the three hundred dollars a month they received to manage the apartment building. Dinner often consisted only of biscuit mix. Or popcorn. There was no job waiting for Bob after he finished his sentence, but Rae was hopeful of getting secretarial work back on campus. Just after the first of the year, Cal's department of environmental design hired her at six hundred a month.

"Now we can get married." She laughed. But she was not joking. She felt he'd need her. He was the only person in the world in 1971 who did depend on her.

"This thing between us hasn't reached what you could call a serious stage," she told a campus friend. "I mean, I didn't wake up one morning and see the sun shining through the window and hear birds singing and know that I was in love with Bob Presley. He didn't either. This has not been a romance. Or a courtship."

He was to be released on January 23. A few days earlier Bob and Rae decided it was a good idea to get married. Neither could cite a specific reason. "It just happened," Rae said. "Everything that ever happened to us just happened."

"I guess I'm gonna marry her," Bob told Blackwell.

Rae put a down payment on a 1967 Cadillac convertible: monthly payments of $120. She picked up Bob at Santa Rita the morning of his release, and they drove to Reno, Nevada. They bought two rings for a total of $15 at a pawnshop, got a marriage license at the Washoe County Courthouse, walked to a storefront wedding shop, paid $12 for a ceremony, single carnation, photograph, and tape recording of the nuptial consummation, and then drove down the Sierra to Oakland, where Rae had recently rented a $140-a-month apartment. Somewhere in the mountains Rae rolled down the car window and threw the flower and tape recording into a snowbank. She found the entire events of that day, and of her life to that point, amusing.

For the first time in years, Bob was off the merry-go-round. No games, no schedules, no enforced strivings. He had time, if he wished, to consider the shape of his life, to get his bearings, to determine a future. He was twenty-five years old and a newlywed. He was a high school graduate and held a degree of sorts from a junior college. Both just pieces of paper. Within six months he could pick up enough credits to graduate from Cal. He had thought about graduating a year earlier, at the time he was waiting for the check charge litigation to end. In fact, he'd gone to the registrar's office and asked for enrollment forms, but he never filled them out.

"Too much damn paperwork," he told Waddell Black-well, who kept pushing Bob to take enough courses to graduate so that he could compete in the job market. But Bob was not at all confident that he could pass a college course anymore. Especially not without the same kind of tutoring help he'd gotten as an athlete. Not without help from Adriana in taking tests, help from Rae in writing papers, help from coaches and athletic department administrators and instructors who were always delighted to assist a star athlete. When eligibility goes, the perquisites of being a big man on campus vanish, too.

Bob had no idea what kind of work he wanted to do anyway, and so he saw no reason to study and graduate and then compete for a job in which he had no interest. Going back to school would just be a waste of time.

He needed a business. His own business. That was his notion as a kid, and that seemed to make the most sense to him now. He would ask Rae to think of something. He felt if she put her mind to it, she could come up with something, some business for him.

Rae was still working on campus as a secretary to a professor of environmental design, but her paychecks went quickly for rent, food, the payment on Bob's car, and his walking-around money. She was upset with Bob's refusal to find what she called "a real job," and she felt she wasn't getting anywhere on her own. In the first months after the marriage, Rae was persistently depressed. She didn't care how she looked or if the apartment was messy. She went through her daily working routine listlessly. She felt trapped but made no effort to free herself. Often Bob complained about her failure to dust and vacuum and mop and wash the dishes at home.

"Screw you, turkey," she'd tell him. "I can do whatever I want or don't want. I'm paying the goddamn bills, so don't you be telling me what to do."

She felt she had the male role and that Bob was also expecting her to do womanly things—the housework. She didn't mind the male role, but she didn't have the energy to do everything. He responded to her taunts by slugging her.

"Every time I yelled at him about the fact I was making the money, I could count on getting beat sometime in the next day and a half," Rae said.

She didn't know where Bob spent his days. But he was in the apartment when she returned from work late every afternoon, and quite often he'd cleaned the place and made dinner. He told her he'd been seeing old friends, trying to find the "right" job, seeking a good, solid connection. After a while, she wasn't sure if he was telling her the truth.

"I loved him for sure," she said, "but I wasn't certain at that time that I actually *liked* him. There were days I both loved and hated him. At the same time. Maybe that seems dumb, but that's just the way it was right after we got married."

"You better find me somethin'," he said to her one evening. "I'm leavin' it up to you. You must know somebody who has a business for me."

"Sure." She scowled. "How about Rockefeller. Or the president of Bank of America. Maybe Howard Hughes. I'll just call all of 'em first thing in the morning and tell them that Bob Presley has finally decided to join their organizations. How much you want for starting salary? Ten thou a week? Or you wanna hold out for bonuses and free stock and a company car?"

"Cut the shit, woman," Bob said, and he grabbed her right arm. They were seated on the couch, a slatted wooden affair covered with pillows.

"Let go, turkey," Rae hollered.

Bob now was squeezing both of her upper arms in his hands. She brought up a foot and kicked away two of the pillows that covered the slats on the back of the couch. Then she grabbed his head with her hands and began banging it against the boards. He continued to squeeze her arms, but he did not make a move for her hands. He was letting her hurt him. When she realized he wasn't going to resist, she released her grip on his head. He immediately let go of her arms and stood up.

"Hey, Slim, just get me a business, huh? Just help me. I need you to help me. Can't you see that?"

Rae nodded. "OK," she promised. "I'll ask around." She was amazed that he hadn't thrashed her but was not of a mind to test him again. She was needed, and at the moment that was the primary consideration. "It might take some time," she warned, "but I'll do what I can."

"I know you will, Slim. I know you always try for me."

Those words, Rae felt, were about as close as Bob could come to affection. She thought to herself: a gorilla in a field of daisies. She smiled, and Bob whacked her gently on the butt.

Rae's business contacts in the Eastbay were not as broad as Bob's. He had the name, but unfortunately, by now, also a reputation. Yet his image as a potential "bad-ass" had not totally rubbed off on her; actually, some of their closest friends were not aware, or were not positively certain, that Bob and Rae were married. Some people on the street thought that Rae was just one of Presley's women. Others knew her as his current, main woman. She was resented by a few of the blacks who'd known Bob since his first days in Berkeley—either because of her whiteness or her wisecracks. Once a black activist came to the Presleys' apartment. Another couple, both black, were already there when the activist arrived. Bob and Rae had known the man for nearly three years. When he walked in, he said hello to Bob and to the other couple, but he ignored Rae—just sat down and began talking to the other couple.

"Say hello to Rae," Bob told the activist, who did not stop his conversation.

"I told you, man, to say hello to Rae." Bob's voice now was louder. He hovered over the guest. "Right now."

The activist, very carefully so that he would not appear patronizing, stood up, looked directly at Rae, and said, "Hi, Rae. How you doin'?" She told him that she was doing just fine and passed him a glass of wine. Bob's powers of intimidation never lagged, but he couldn't put them to any practical use. Rae was his connection to reality.

When she'd first moved from San Jose to Berkeley, Rae had worked part-time for an Oakland tailor. She saw the man every now and then after she quit working for him; they'd remained personal friends, but until now she had never asked him for a favor. The tailor,

Mike, knew all about Bob's background yet had never pumped Rae for information beyond what he'd read in the papers or heard on the street. Mike accepted Rae and thus evinced an unstated acceptance of Bob.

"What can Bob do?" Mike asked after Rae told him she was ferreting for "any kind of business" for Presley.

"Well, he does know clothes," she said. "He could probably be a designer of men's clothes if he had a little training. His instincts on style are really sharp."

"But if I had him come in with me," noted Mike, "it wouldn't really be his business. He'd be working for me just like you worked for me. Could he handle that? Can he take orders?"

"Maybe if you were an NBA coach, he could." She smiled. "Or owned a pro franchise."

"I get the drift," Mike said. "Tell you what. I'll talk to some real estate people I know and see what's available."

"You understand," warned Rae, "that what I'm looking for is something for nothing. Somebody who needs a manager. Or maybe a lease option deal on a going operation. We are not what you call heavily capitalized. We are not, in fact, capitalized period."

Mike admitted to Rae that he would feel more at ease if he knew that she would be involved in whatever he came up with.

"Sure," said Rae. "I have nothing to do after my eight-hour-a-day job anyway. Just go ahead and use my stamina for collateral."

"Give me a few weeks, Rae. You'll hear from me."

Eight days later Mike telephoned Rae and asked her to meet him after work in the bar at Trader Vic's on San Pablo Avenue in Oakland. When she got there, Mike laid out a proposition. Across the street from Vic's—Rae

had often passed the place but had never been inside—
was a crusty old neighborhood bar called the Monkey's
Paw. Neither the bar nor its location had much merit.
In fact, the only spot in that neighborhood with any
notoriety was Vic's, the original restaurant in what had
become a national operation.

"I know the owner of the Paw," said Mike. "He has
no interest in running it himself anymore. He doesn't
even care about owning it. The place just doesn't do that
much business and I think he'd sell it in a minute if he
could, except he's been looking for a year and can't find
a buyer. Or anyone to even lease the damn place. I told
him about you and Bob. Told him you were hardwork-
ing kids who wanted to get started in something of their
own but that you didn't have a penny to invest. And
together we came up with a deal I think you'll like."

Mike's proposal was perfect from Rae's point of view;
she knew it would appeal to Bob, too. The owner of the
Monkey's Paw was going to let them run the place for
four months. They would have to assume all of the overhead themselves. He'd take it off the market in that time
period, and if after the four months the Presleys wanted
to buy the bar, he'd work out an easy mortgage payment
plan: nothing down, so much a month. The owner figured that the young couple might do well enough to
take the place off his hands and provide him with a
modest monthly income.

"Sounds like a swell white elephant sale," Rae said
in explaining the deal to Bob. "But it'll take a lot of
work. You've gotta realize that going in. I'm willing if
you are."

He asked how soon they could take over. That was all
he said. But it was sufficient to convince her that he was
eager to get started.

She didn't necessarily share his enthusiasm; the Monkey's Paw would mean more work for her. She was pleased for Bob and depressed for herself. But she believed that if the bar did well, she could quit her job at Cal and then either "retire" or just spend a few hours a day working at the Paw with Bob. At least now there was an opportunity, a little hope.

In the month before they officially opened the bar, Rae saved enough money—and delayed paying their apartment utility and phone bills—to buy sufficient stock for the bar, which was licensed to serve only beer and wine. She planned to buy enough inventory to last for four or five days and then use the receipts from those first days, on the assumption there would indeed be receipts, to buy more beer and wine.

Meanwhile, before the Presleys opened for business, Bob spent several hours a day cleaning and painting the Paw. He decided on a decor of yellow and black, got the paint on credit, and was able to scrounge scraps of lumber which he used to patch together a back bar. When he wasn't sprucing up the Paw, he was on campus or on Telegraph Avenue passing the word to friends that he was about to open a bar and inviting them to drop in for a drink.

"It's good PR," he told Rae. "Good for business."

"It's also good for business not to give away too many beers," she said.

"I believe," he said, "that whatever I give away you can win back on the pool table in the place." Rae did shoot a good stick.

"Whatever's right," Bob said.

"Profitable is righter." Rae laughed. "I can always sleep in my next life."

"Just get it done in seventy-one." Bob giggled. "No flaw at the Paw."

But it didn't work: people didn't come, expenses were

too high, the neighborhood was bad. Bob considered the
Monkey's Paw experience another personal failure. He'd
had the chance, another chance, and he'd failed. That
was his track record: a failure in ball, a failure in crime,
a failure in business. He was convinced he couldn't do
anything well, or half well. After the Paw closed, he
didn't leave the apartment for two weeks. He stayed
inside and cleaned and cooked.

His only current asset, as always, was his size. He
knew those seven feet were the last, the only resort for
him. And it was unlikely he would get another chance
in ball because nobody would take a chance on a guy
with his background of failure. Rae would have to be
his meal ticket, as usual, until he got a break, but Bob
didn't think he'd ever get another break. In anything.

Bob had not reckoned, though, with the indirect loy-
alty of a University of California alumnus and sports
enthusiast named Bob Bell, known around the campus
community as "Berkeley Bob."

There's a Bob Bell at every major college in the
country: a former athlete turned successful businessman
turned athletic department angel. "Berkeley Bob," who
had been an outstanding high school athlete in Berkeley,
had his college athletic career cut short by injury. Bell
now owned an auto-leasing agency and auto sales dis-
tributorship in Berkeley. He and his family had a large
home, complete with swimming pool and basketball
court, in the Berkeley hills.

More than most who are obsessed with organized
athletics, Bob Bell understood people as well as games.
He had played, coached, and scouted basketball. He had
grown up in the Berkeley ghetto; he was a street-wise
white; among his closest friends was Bill Russell, who'd

come out of the ghetto in Oakland. Bell knew the problems of the ghetto youngster who found himself in college because of his sports ability, and he always tried to help a struggling, sincere kid, either with a few bucks or with a job at one of his businesses.

Bell met Presley when Bob first came to Cal, met him through Waddell Blackwell, whom the older man respected and liked. He accepted Presley because Presley was Waddell's friend.

"Presley came to Cal with big eyes," Bell reminisced, "as if somebody had told him, 'OK, it's your turn to get whatever you want. We're black, and it's our turn.' But Presley would have been cooperative here if a good salesman had handled him. If Padgett had wanted to cooperate with Herrerias, he could have told Presley to go *bald* and Presley would have gone bald. Bob was highly overrated as a ballplayer. And he wasn't prepared for the college environment. Nobody helped him adapt. And he couldn't help himself. You can't help someone who won't help themselves. Presley just didn't have the things inside him to live in this society. He felt the world abused him. But he wasn't dumb. It's just that he couldn't put all the pieces together."

Bell went out of his way to help Bob. Not for Cal. Nor for Bob Presley. But because Waddell asked Bell to help Presley.

"He was Waddell's friend," said Bell, "so I did what I could for him. I guess there's a weakness in my character that makes me help people when they ask. Maybe I thought I was a priest. Or a lecturer."

Back in early 1970, while Bob was awaiting trial on the check charge, he twice asked Waddell to ask Bell for assistance. The first time, Bell gave Presley a job washing cars in his leasing garage, but Presley felt he wasn't getting enough money and stopped showing up for work after a few days.

Then a few months later, Waddell again came to Bell on Presley's behalf. Bell had a friend who ran a scavenger service in Richmond, and he got Bob hired on as a truck driver's assistant. But Presley stayed in the garbage business for only one shift. At day's end he told the driver, "Man, you guys are crazy. This work is too hard. I'm not gonna do this."

Finally, in mid-spring 1971, after the demise of the Monkey's Paw, Waddell again approached Bell to plead for another opportunity for Presley, preferably something in basketball somewhere.

Bell had a connection in Manila. One of the teams in the professional basketball league in the Philippines, a club owned by a Manila utility company, was looking for a big man. Bell told his Manila contact about Presley and worked out a contract with one phone call.

"If you're straight over there," Bell told Bob, "you'll be OK. Just because the world's screwed up doesn't mean you should be. Hey, man, learn to cope. And just remember that there's more to life than making a basket."

Bob listened courteously to Bell. "He was always polite to me," Bell said, "because I was Waddell's friend."

By June 1971, Bob and Rae were in Manila.

11

MANY AMERICAN BALLPLAYERS who don't land slots on U.S. pro teams turn to the leagues overseas for both economic and artistic reasons: the pay is not bad, and a player can stay in shape and polish his game in the hope that the NBA will want to look at him the following year. Presley saw his opportunity in Manila more in terms of monetary salvation. He went from the ranks of the unemployed to a job that would pay him expenses plus a thousand dollars a month at the start and two thousand a month before the season ended in late summer. Bob and Rae were given a rent-free villa with a free maid and free cook, and a chauffeured Mercedes was always at their disposal.

Bob had little trouble looking good in the games because most of the players were small. And he quickly drew the attention of Manila groupies. "Neither the women nor the athletes were very discreet," said Rae.

She was extremely jealous. "Here I was enjoying this newlywed, happily married syndrome," she complained, "and here Bob was going to a party without me after a game or trying to send me home with another guy. He'd keep telling me, 'It's nothing personal.' And it took me years to realize he really meant that." But the relative luxury of their life in Manila kept Rae satisfied and generally happy with her relationship. She was living like a lady. "I didn't even mind the lizards and the humidity," she said. "And every meal our cook made was perfect. We kept trying to find something to complain about, but really couldn't. After one meal, Bob said, 'It'll be great to get back home and have you burn some eggs.' "

They came back to the United States with about six thousand dollars saved by season's end. Bob talked of using the money to start some kind of business.

Late in 1971 Rae took a job as a legal secretary in Oakland. Bob spent his days playing ball in gyms and rec centers in the Eastbay and talked of getting a tryout with a pro club. "Manila was OK," he told Rae, "but it's not the NBA. If I stay in shape, I can make it."

There were evenings he wouldn't come home; Rae guessed he was seeing other women but did not know that one of them was Adriana. And Bob was unaware that Rae occasionally got together with one of her old hundred-dollar-a-night dates. But the marriage in that first year was compatible, if unromantic. "Only once," said Rae, "did he ever tell me he loved me. We were on the couch watching TV and suddenly he put his arm around me and said, 'I love you, Slim. But don't ever tell anybody I said that.' "

He spent the first few months of 1972 alone in the Philippines for a tournament, came home to Oakland briefly, then returned to Manila in the spring for another season. Again alone. The money was good for him and she enjoyed her own work, so Rae did not object to the separation. She knew about an athlete's life. Separations were inherent to sports.

Bob was flushed with his semblance of success in Manila and passed the word to old friends at Cal that he was truly ready for the pros if only somebody could arrange a tryout. In late summer 1972, Oakland attorney Wayne Hooper, an Old Blue and agent for such prominent athletes as Sal Bando and Jim Plunkett, set up just such an opportunity for Bob with the Miami Floridians of the ABA. Presley returned to the Bay Area before the season ended in Manila so that he could work out contract arrangements; Hooper was able to get him a contract for $42,000 a year—if he made the team. Bob was as enthusiastic as Rae had ever seen him. He was running around Lake Merritt every day. "I'll be in great shape this time," he told her. "I'll run my ass off down there."

Rae wanted to go to the training camp with him, but Bob preferred to go alone. "And if I make the team, I'm gonna stay in Miami by myself, too," he said.

"Hey, look," protested Rae. "I've helped you get this far, and I've reached the point I don't want to stay here alone anymore." But he didn't budge, so Rae took the Cadillac, drove to a girlfriend's apartment, and stayed there until Bob had left for the South.

"I knew," said Rae, "that if he made it, we'd be through. He wouldn't need me anymore. He'd have ball, and he wouldn't need me."

Bob Bass was the Miami coach. He'd been in the

Denver front office early in 1969 and urged the drafting of Presley then. When Hooper called, Bass remembered Bob. Coaches never forget anybody.

The starting Floridian center was Ira Harge, and Bass considered either Presley or Carl Fuller as Harge's backup. Only one of the two would be kept.

Presley's problem during the training camp at the North Miami Community Center and exhibition games was "lack of intensity." Bass pointed to his short concentration span. "He played all out for eight or ten minutes at a stretch and then did nothing; he was completely out of it for four or five plays in a row. Carl Fuller wasn't as talented as Presley, but he played harder."

Bob survived with the Floridians until the last cut. According to him, he was lopped from the roster "for political reasons. They were looking at me and another guy for second-string center," he told Rae, "and the other guy had his wife and kids with him, so they felt sorry for him and kept him instead of me." He confessed to Rae that at the start of the training camp he had lied about his marital status. "Guess I screwed myself," he said.

"When he came home," remembered Rae, "I finally figured out that he'd *never* play pro ball. Not because of his ability necessarily. Or even because of his attitude. But because of his history. I thought his background, his history, would have a permanent detrimental effect on any future he desired."

He was in Oakland only a few weeks before he decided to go to Europe and try to catch on with a pro club there. He spent a week in Belgium but did not make the team. "I was outa shape," he alibied to Rae, who knew he was in the best physical condition she'd ever seen him.

They observed Christmas 1972 by renting a house on Twenty-sixth Avenue in Oakland and trading in their 1967 Cadillac convertible for a 1971 Caddy Coupe De Ville, with monthly payments of $180.

Bob no longer talked exclusively about ball. He took the balance of his savings from his Manila salary and bought a restaurant on Ocean Avenue in San Francisco. Rae had the feeling Bob wanted to place as much distance between himself and ball as he could: "Like he'd put the brakes on and said, 'Stop.'"

Bob worked long hours at his drive-in restaurant in San Francisco. The previous owners were Filipinos. Their menu featured dishes of their native land, but when Bob took over, he turned the place into a hamburger joint. A cousin in San Francisco, Shelley Hart, taught Bob and Rae how to make french fries. Rae came to the drive-in most evenings after putting in a full day at her law office. This cut down on expenses, but even with the low overhead, the place was failing.

"You got to be silly thinking that all of those Orientals in your neighborhood are gonna rush down to eat your cooking," Waddell told Bob. And there was a competitive problem: a McDonald's only two blocks away.

Bob operated the drive-in until late 1973, when his lease and savings ran out. He was not particularly bitter about the business failure. "Somethin' else'll come along," he promised Rae.

She was not so sure. She was getting fed up with Bob's dreams of business or basketball success. She was weary, after the restaurant closed, of being the only provider.

Bob spent his unemployed days of early 1974 driving around in the Caddy, visiting friends, or playing ball in a park in Berkeley's civic center. One evening when she was permitted to use the car, Rae drove it to the dealer's and simply turned it in; she didn't want to be harnessed with the $180 monthly payments, and she was so disgusted with Bob's idleness that she didn't even ask the dealer for the equity they had in the car. When she told him what she'd done, Bob moved out.

One of the men with whom he played ball in the Berkeley park was Bill Belford, a basketball fixture in the Eastbay for a quarter century. Belford came out of Oakland's McClymonds High School a year before Bill Russell started playing there. Belford was a father figure to blacks in the area of Merritt Junior College. He operated a small diner under the BART tracks near the Oakland-Berkeley line. He also sponsored a basketball team that played weekends in Richmond and San Francisco. His diner was called the Believers, as was his team. Belford found a place for Presley in both enterprises in spring 1974. Bob was fry cook on the night shift at the diner and started at center for the Believers ball club.

There was no money in the weekend games. "But sometimes NBA scouts come by," Belford said. "George Johnson played for me. Some of the Warriors' folks came to watch him, and that's how he made it into the NBA."

Presley had heard similar tempting notions when he'd joined a semipro team in the suburb of Martinez for the end of the 1973–74 season. George Johnson, the Warriors' reserve center, once played in that league, too.

Bob and Belford talked in the late evenings at the

diner. Belford came in to work on the books and check on supplies. Bob said little during Belford's visits. "You enjoy yourself only when you're playing ball, don't you?" said Belford one evening. There was no response.

"Seems to me," prompted Belford, "the best time for you is when you're playing against a guy just as big."

Bob agreed. "If the other center is tall, it's good for me. But there are games when their center's a little guy that I just can't get nothing out of it."

"You got great talent," Belford told him, "if you only put out all the time. Like in some games you don't seem to care if you play ball well or not. And if you're not playing hard on a night a pro scout shows up, what'll they think? Don't you want them to see you doing well?"

Bob didn't answer.

"You keep telling me that you think you're good enough to make the pros right now. You keep saying you want the scouts to see you. You want to make it quick, right away, but you won't put out."

There was silence for a minute. Belford was about to tell Bob good night when Bob motioned for the older man to sit down at the counter. Bob dropped a quarter into the jukebox and punched half a Carmen McRae album. He spoke over her.

"Nobody's gonna scout me," Bob said. There was no anger, no animation. Belford never got over how such a big man spoke so evenly.

"All the pro teams are alike," Bob continued. "The pros are like a syndicate: a bunch of individual owners, sure, but all in one syndicate. None of them want me. They all got the message—lay off Presley, he's trouble."

"Look," replied Belford, "everybody knows you messed up once. But you can outlive that. You can work hard in the game. If you keep working hard, they'll know. People are out there needing a big man, and if you put out, the word will get around. The thing with you is that you got to work harder than everybody just because you messed up before. But you can do it. You got to try."

Bob leaned back on the counter and listened to Carmen. He's turned me off, Belford thought. He's with you for a while and then he turns you off, doesn't want to listen anymore.

"I've had so much trouble in my life, Bill. So much that sometimes I don't care about anything. I don't think I have any use for living. That's how it is sometimes."

"It's not your choice," Bill said. "You can't say you got no use for living. You don't put yourself here and you can't take yourself away."

One of Bob's teammates on the Believers was Robert Scotlan, a six-foot, seven-inch former University of San Diego basketball player who worked in the family maintenance business about a mile from Belford's diner. Scotlan was two years younger than Presley and had first met Bob at Cal. Later, they ran into each other at pickup games in gyms and parks, two members of a large community of college-honed blacks in their twenties who passed the time playing ball on both sides of the Bay. Everybody knew everybody else—casually.

Scotlan shared Bob's good feelings about Belford, but both complained about one of Belford's coaching gambits: putting down his players in hopes of inspiring them. Usually, Belford just made them mad.

Driving back from games, Belford told Bob, "You'd better get yourself a little ball and squeeze it a hundred times a day. You're awful weak for a big man." Because Belford's barbs were directed at all of his players, Bob could smile at them—most of the time. But often he was hurt.

"You're a bad basketball player," Belford said in the car one evening. "You'd be better off washing dishes."

During a game, Belford made a substitution Bob could not quite fathom. While running up and down the court, Bob yelled to Belford on the bench. And Belford shouted back, "You're stupid, Presley. That's why you're not playing in the pros now. You're a dummy." Scotlan and the other guys laughed and tried to concentrate on the game. The other team was only confused.

"Don't let Belford get you down," Scotlan advised Bob after a game one evening. "He's just trying to motivate you. He doesn't mean anything by it."

"I understand that," said Bob. "But I can get down on myself without him. It's getting too late for me. I don't think anybody would take me now in the pros."

"You're capable, though," said Scotlan. "You're in real good shape. You can play the game. So don't get down on yourself about your talent, man. You got the talent. But you got to remember there's all kinds of talent out there. There's too many pretty good college players and too few jobs in the pros. Hey, just think of the players in this country who are seven feet tall and who nobody's ever heard of. They're out there, man, and they're unknown and not playing."

Bob and Scotlan ran down the list of second-string centers in the NBA. They'd watch a televised game and discuss how second-rate most of the reserve big men looked. "You're better than that bunch right now," Scotlan said. "And you're probably as good as some of those centers who are starting. You just got to keep improving; work on the left-handed hook; move better to your left. You keep working and you can forget the second-string stuff, man. If you get good enough, there are some teams you can *start* for."

Bob nodded. He'd been thinking about the teams that needed a big man. Maybe Portland. Maybe Phoenix. If he could only get them to take a look at him.

Scotlan didn't say so, but he wondered if anybody would look at Presley. The unspoken line, the way Scotlan heard it kicked around, was that Bob had a label, that he was "a head problem who couldn't get along with anybody." Scotlan didn't know if Bob could shed that old label.

12

By late 1974 Bob was tired of working nights at Belford's. Scotlan said there was a job available at his family's place, so Bob quit the Believers and became a telephone booth maintenance man, which meant he scrubbed and vacuumed phone booths. The job paid over $4 an hour; every two weeks Bob netted about $280. He was not happy with the money but felt at least he was working days and could spend more time with his dogs—Rae had bought another—and his plants and, once again, with Rae. He filled the house with several dozen small pots and a variety of greens. He'd pot and repot and then plant and transplant. Scotlan chuckled whenever Bob picked up a loose limb from the street and said he'd take it home and make it grow.

The Scotlan maintenance operation had been going for thirty years. Robert's father, George, hired mostly friends. He had a valuable contract with Pacific Telephone to maintain thousands of their booths in three separate counties in the Bay Area. A two-man crew cleaned fifty a day; the company maintained an average of almost seven thousand booths each month. Each crew had a daily route, starting at 6:00 A.M., and worked until the route was finished, usually mid-afternoon. Often the crews also worked in apartment buildings, cleaning flats before rental. The work was hard, the atmosphere rather loose. At the end of his shift, Bob played dominoes or cards in the company garage before catching his bus to the other side of Oakland. He appeared comfortable, although he was restless about wanting to play ball in a place where it mattered. Everybody at Scotlan's accepted him. Bob just did his work and didn't have to explain anything to anybody.

Bob and Robert Scotlan were riding down an outside elevator one morning and spotted a man on the ground staring at them. The man yelled up, "Hey, big man, how tall are you?"

"Aw, shit," said Bob. "I'm seven foot eight," he shouted. The stranger, now face to face with them, was angry as the elevator reached bottom.

"How much you weigh, man?" countered Presley. And the stranger turned and walked away. "Son of a bitch," said Bob.

"I can clown with these cats," observed Scotlan, "but still sometimes it gets to me the way it gets to you. I mean, we're not supposed to ask fat people how fat they are or skinny people how much they weigh or ugly people how ugly they are. But everybody thinks it's OK to ask a big man how tall he is."

Bob's regular crew partner was an older man, Johnny Moore. Johnny told Scotlan that Bob's work was just fine, except when it came to cleaning phone booths at the Oakland airport. A booth is about six feet, eight inches tall. Bob had to duck when he went inside with the squeegee and vacuum. "Why don't they build these damn doors higher?" he'd say to Johnny Moore. In the airport booths, Bob made himself as small as he could once inside. Moore told Bob he'd do the inside, but Presley insisted. He didn't want to be noticed in a busy public place cleaning the outside of telephone booths. Somebody he knew might see him. Booths on street corners or in gas stations were OK; people were driving by fast and couldn't see him. But the airport was different. In the airport it was better to be uncomfortable, and hidden.

"Maybe I should go back home," Bob mused to Robert Scotlan one afternoon over dominoes. "Maybe it'd be easier for me back there in Detroit. My brother tells me things aren't good at home for jobs, but maybe I can find something. Maybe the thing I should do is get a black wife. Rae's really helped me out. You know that. But sometimes I think a strong black woman might help me better along the way. I've been thinking about that."

Bob and Scotlan were both involved in the Western Basketball Association in the 1974–75 season. The WBA began in 1970 as a casual semipro weekend league in a handful of Northern California cities. By 1974 the owners of the league's teams hoped the WBA could become a pure minor league operation for the NBA. Fresh money came into the league, which now had six teams.

Dale Hall, a forty-seven-year-old white, ran the Martinez Muirs. He had spent most of his life in sports. His brother-in-law was "Berkeley Bob" Bell. Like Bell, Hall had coached a variety of subcollege basketball teams, but Hall did not have Bell's affluence; Dale's only income came from a job as a programmer with Kaiser Aerospace.

He had needed a center late in the previous season but wasn't certain he wanted a player with Bob's emotional credentials. "You have a reputation for blowing your cool," he pointed out.

"I know," Bob admitted. "I know I've got to keep myself under control at all times. I was immature when I pulled all that shit at Cal. That was a long time ago. I can give you some good minutes on the court."

But Bob didn't play well in his first shot with Martinez. Hall wondered if Presley was smoking too much dope in the locker room. The odor was always there, and Hall didn't think Bob was the only offender. This new breed of athlete confused Dale Hall.

When Hall offered Bob a chance to play with the Muirs in 1974–75, he insisted that Presley come in clean: in good shape, a minimum of joints, a good attitude.

"I want you on my team," said Dale, "but remember that Martinez is my hometown. I'm in the Exchange Club in Martinez. I've lived in Martinez for fifteen years. I know that you don't mess around all that much with pot or coke. I know it's no big problem for you because I've asked around. All I ask is that you keep it out of the gym and don't embarrass me or the team or the town."

Bob guaranteed Hall there would be no trouble. He moved in with Rae in a rented house on Murdock Court in East Oakland. She could see his renewed enthusiasm. "Not many people give a shit about me," he said. "No white people except Dale Hall." He told Rae the stories about NBA scouts coming to WBA games. The George Johnson story. She'd heard them all.

"You've got potential," Hall told him by midseason.

"Maybe somebody in the NBA will want you after we finish in March. If you keep playing well, I'll talk to some people. Stu Inman of Portland has asked me to look out for talent. He needs power forwards, but he might be interested in looking at a center. So keep giving it your best, and we'll see."

Scotlan coached the San Jose team in the WBA. Whenever his Winchesters played the Muirs, he noted Presley's air of confidence on the court. Yet at work Bob appeared unsure and often pessimistic about a future in ball. At Christmas time in 1974, during a break in WBA play, Bob took time off from Scotlan's to visit the family in Detroit.

The Presleys' small house was crowded. Edna had become a mother to a two-year-old and a one-year-old, the children of her youngest daughter, Denise. The Presleys did not know where she was living; they had an idea how she was living.

Bob told them he was only going to stay for a week. He did not bring them presents. He phoned Rae every evening. He went to a shopping center with two of his sisters and bought Rae a sixty-dollar pair of boots. "You could see," said Edna, "he really wanted to get on back to Rae."

Edna wanted him to talk, but she knew she couldn't force conversation. She had left her job as a cook at the Catholic diocese and was now home all day on Wyoming Street, caring for Denise's children full-time. She rarely left the house. She had no interest in seeing anyone other than her children and grandchildren. When she wasn't cooking or cleaning, she sat in an overstuffed chair in an alcove between the living room and dining room and talked on the telephone with one daughter or another. Edna was reclusive. She wanted it that way.

His second afternoon in Detroit, Bob was alone in the house with Edna. He was ready to talk. The conversation was mostly about basketball. He reviewed his career for her, repeatedly asking, "Do you think I can make it, Mama?" He didn't wait for an answer.

"I keep failin'," he said. "Failin' with Rae, failin' with basketball. Neither one of them is any good for me. But maybe I'll be goin' back to big-time ball. Goin' up. You think I'll make it, Mama?"

When he finally paused, Edna said, "If you're failing, you're failing yourself. You can't blame Rae or ball. It's you that's failing." She told him that if things didn't work out for him in ball soon, he should consider coming back to Detroit.

"I don't wanna come back here with less than I left with," he said. "I shouldn't even be in Detroit now. But since you've left the old neighborhood and nobody around here knows me, I came." Then he switched to basketball.

"I know I can make it. This is my whole life. My whole aim. I can't let all this ball go down the drain. I don't wanna come back here and work in no auto factory or steel mill. I can't come back. I got to make it. I *got* to make it. Do you think I can make it, Mama? If you say I can make it, well, you're usually right, so I can make it."

"Listen," Edna said, "if you don't make it in basketball or in California, you'll make it in some other job in some other place. Why is ball so important?"

But Bob didn't answer her. All he said was, "I have to make it out there where I am. I have to."

When Robert came home from Ford that evening, Edna pulled him aside and said, "I've never heard one

man talk about ball so much in my life. Oooh, but I'm
tired hearing all about that ball. Anybody talkin' about
ball that much, you'd think their mind is gone."

The balance of the WBA season was a good one for
Bob. He ran around Lake Merritt every day to stay in
shape. He smoked dope only while riding to games with
a teammate. He averaged about twenty points and fourteen rebounds. He went all-out to earn his $25 a game.
The players were also supposed to share in receipts at
the Saturday and Sunday games, but there were no receipts to split. Dale Hall lost $3,500 in the 1974–75 sea-
son; the league itself dropped nearly $30,000.

The season ended on March 16, 1975. Hall told Presley he'd soon be in contact with Inman in Portland.
Hall was sincere about making the contact. He told Bob
he'd wait until the NBA regular season was over in
April. "I'll let you know," he said. Bob hoped he'd
know soon.

On Telegraph Avenue in Berkeley one early March
afternoon, Bob spotted Nick Peters, the sports editor of
the *Berkeley Gazette*. He hadn't seen Peters in a few
years—not since Nick gave him a brief shot at sports-
writing. He'd had Bob try a few stories, but they were
neither well written nor well crafted. As nicely as possible, Nick told Presley to work on his writing and try
again another time.

They had a Coke at Kip's, a campus hangout, and Bob
told Peters he had been playing well and might finally
be given another look by the pros.

"The way I look at it," Bob said, "is that the system
gave me an opportunity to play ball once, and I just
wasn't ready for it. I know I was a pain in the neck to a

lot of people here in Berkeley. I know I should have cut my hair. If I'd known then what I know now, I would have cut my hair *every day* at Cal. But what I did then I thought was right. I was black and I was big. I was like a central figure. So I couldn't cut my hair. I don't know if you dig, but I just couldn't. Not then."

Peters nodded. "You were too visible."

"At that time, it was right," said Bob. "It just seemed the right thing to do. But in the long run it wasn't worth the hassle. I just couldn't see what that would do to me. I didn't have the sense to understand what was happening and what would happen. I didn't have anyone to set me straight. I was just a big, dumb kid out of the ghetto, and I was expected to adjust to this big place here overnight. And I couldn't do it. But shit, Nick, if I only knew what was at stake."

"Your WBA numbers look pretty good this year," observed Peters.

"You know, I think I'm finally ready for the system," Presley went on. "After all this time. But now that I'm ready, the system ain't ready for me. The system won't let me play. I'm really motivated now, too. I still think I can make it."

"You really think so?"

"Yeah, I honestly do. I'm going to give it one more year. I wish I could have done it all differently. But it doesn't do any good to look back. I just hope I can make it pretty soon. I've got to do it soon."

On Monday, March 17, Rae started a new job in San Francisco. She was still a legal secretary but now earned more money, nearly $800 a month, a raise of about $150. It was more expensive commuting to San Francisco than to downtown Oakland, but the raise made the job change worthwhile.

Bob estimated she was earning at least fifty bucks a week more than he made at Scotlan's. Her enthusiasm bugged him. Not that he wasn't kind of happy for her. She did work hard and she was smart, and he knew there was no reason she shouldn't get ahead, but it just didn't seem right that she should be making all that much more than he. From the moment two weeks earlier when she'd told him about the new job possibility, he was resentful. He didn't say anything then; he didn't want to start another big argument.

Everything had been cool since he moved out of Belford's place and back with Rae the previous fall. There were the usual uneasy moments, but the two of them would never have calm. He knew that and felt she did, too. Once in talking to Rae about his family and arguments between his mother and father, Bob mused, "I guess we'll be just like my parents. They finally seem to have it all together after twenty-six years. So you and me, we'll fight and fuss for about thirty years and then we'll get it together."

Still, Bob wondered why Rae kept the marriage alive. What the hell did she need him for? What the hell was he good for?

Waddell Blackwell told him to stop thinking that way, to drop what Waddell called "ghetto fatalism—asking yourself all the time, 'Why should I do this? Why should I try that? It doesn't matter because nothing's going to work out. So nothing matters.'"

But Bob saw himself as nothing but a common laborer and Rae as a big-shot legal secretary making enough money to be the man of the house. She didn't flaunt it;

lucky she didn't, he said. But, *damn*, it was getting to him.

On the bus ride to Scotlan's this Monday morning Bob was grim. He couldn't stop thinking about Rae's new money. He wished the WBA season wasn't over. He wished Dale Hall had talked to Stu Inman in Portland. He again wished he were back home. It might all be better back in Detroit. If nothing worked out in Portland, the thing to do was go home. That was his resolve as he and Johnny Moore began their day's rounds in the Datsun pickup.

On her way to work, Rae computed how her raise might make things easier. She was paying the two hundred dollars a month rent for the Murdock Court house and for clothing, incidentals, and utilities.

Bob bought the food out of his salary at Scotlan's. He did not, however, give her money for any other bills, and the food he bought was not that expensive. For several months Bob had been on a vegetarian–health food kick; he baked his own bread and ate an abundance of fruits and nuts. Most evenings he had dinner waiting for Rae when she came home from the law office. He enjoyed doing the cooking, and she appreciated being spared the chore. Not that she didn't fancy cooking herself. She was physically unable to bear children, but Rae wanted nothing more than to be a happy homemaker for a happy family. She knew it sounded silly to some of her friends, but she saw a simplicity in that life-style she envied.

As it was, she and Bob were homebodies. They had made no close friends together. During the few parties to which they'd be invited, Bob always found a corner with the guys and Rae roamed around introducing herself. He showed no interest in meeting new people. "You're too closed off," she told him. "Let yourself out a little." She often wanted to invite people she knew to dinner but was worried that they might "get freaked out on his height."

Her closest friend, Sue Steinpreis, invited the Presleys to dinner one evening. Aside from a "hello," Bob said nothing, and he and Rae went home as soon as the meal was finished. Rae told Sue that Bob wasn't feeling well, was having some problems. Sue wondered if she herself hadn't been at fault. "I hardly feel qualified to talk to him about anything," she said. "And everything always seems so touchy with you two. I know where you're coming from, so maybe I should find out where Bob's coming from. What do you think?"

Rae passed it off. She believed Bob didn't want to open himself up to anybody. "Hell it's too *personal* for him to tell someone, 'I'm feeling fine,' " she said to Sue.

Sue always was in awe of his size. "It doesn't wear off," she explained to Rae. "Even after you've seen him a few times, it still doesn't wear off. He's such a *big* man."

Rae was more convinced than ever that a quiet life at home in the evenings was the most judicious course to follow. Although she was happier being out with people, she tried to please Bob, but her feeling of being stifled increased.

One morning earlier in the year she'd awakened in tears and quietly walked into the kitchen to have a cup of coffee. She tried to calm herself but couldn't. The crying continued. There was so much bothering her: back bills, the lack of company, the nagging repetition of

Bob's conversation about making it in the NBA. The house was starting to smell "like gym socks," she told him. He'd converted the back rooms into a sort of gym, with slant board and barbells, and worked out every day for several hours.

Bob came into the kitchen, saw her anguish, said nothing, walked out of the house. Three hours later, he returned and asked her to come into the dining room. "Just sit down there at the table and don't talk," he ordered. "If you say anything, I'll kill you." She was silent. "Don't do that to me, that crying, ever again. Your crying messes me up. I'm trying to concentrate and put all my energy into basketball. I don't have time to deal with your emotional problems. Don't bother me with them." He left the dining room, changed into a sweat suit, and went to work out in the back.

There were times when Bob admitted to himself that he was limiting Rae's life. When he was busy playing ball at Martinez, he often told her to go out and enjoy herself, and so Rae and Sue went to a bar at which there was live music, had a few drinks, casually danced with whomever seemed interesting, and then split. From the moment he'd tell Rae to take a night out until the moment she came home, Bob fretted. He knew she was with Sue or another girlfriend. He knew he had no reason to believe she was messing around on him. But he refused to believe his common sense. He sat and waited, imagining a variety of liaisons, fantasizing her picking up dudes, wondering where she was from hour to hour. It wasn't that Bob wanted company; he just wanted Rae *there,* with him. Not even to talk. Just there.

She'd come home, never after 1:00 A.M. at the latest, to find an entirely different man than she'd left earlier in the evening. He'd be belligerent. He'd shout, "You're doing everybody in Oakland, woman."

When she bowled one evening a week in Alameda in a men's scratch league—her ability was far above the women's leagues—Bob told her he was convinced she was making it with every man in the league. She said she was too busy bowling, that there wasn't time to mess with even one man.

Rae attributed Bob's anger to his constant frustration about basketball. She tried to contend with it, just as she did with the times he hit her. She was a convenient target; she was always there. She sensed his persistent anger but did not believe it was aimed at whites or at her. She was available, that's all. Bob never apologized after the physical arguments. A day or so later, though, he made an extra-nice dinner for her.

When he did talk to her at length, it was nearly always about ball, about the NBA dream. She tried now to turn him off; the single note was bugging her.

"I listen to this fanatical conversation about making it in the pros, and I want to yell 'Stop' at him," she told Sue Steinpreis. "But I can't. It's his whole life. I can't take that away."

For several years Sue had resented Bob Presley because of the effect she thought he had on Rae. Sue was not accustomed to seeing a woman as the family bread-winner and money manager, as Rae was. "He doesn't do much of anything," she complained. "You do every-thing in the marriage; you'd do anything to keep it going. He's made you submerge your personality, and he's stuck you with debts and then sometimes he hits you. What the hell are you doing staying with him, woman?"

Each time the Presleys split up, Sue told Rae it was futile to go back. She knew that Rae was remembering the college days, a time that was unrecoverable. After the occasional beatings, Rae always called Sue and asked to come over. "I'm leaving him," said Rae.

"It makes no sense for the two of you to stay together," Sue always advised. Sue believed that if Rae could only stay away from Bob—would move out—for a few months, she'd lose the emotional need to keep the marriage together. A divorce, in Sue's mind, was the best thing; Rae could be her own person; Bob could learn to make it on his own. But the separations never lasted more than two or three days.

"I know it's not right," admitted Rae. "I know I shouldn't be there with him. But . . ."

"But **you** love him, right?"

And Rae agreed that she did.

That Monday evening, when Rae came home after her first day on the new job, Bob was in the kitchen making dinner. Rae wondered why he was wearing her sweater.

Robert Scotlan had quickly put together a team to play in the Martin Luther King Tournament up in Vallejo that week. Scotlan's team had entered the same tourney, a minor regional event sponsored by the Vallejo Recreation Department, the year before and finished second. This year, having a big man might make the difference, Scotlan hoped. So he asked Presley to play.

Bob was frustrated that the WBA season was over, but this thing in Vallejo would kill some time until Hall called Inman in Portland. Bob wished Hall wouldn't wait until the NBA season ended to make the call.

Scotlan picked Bob up at home and didn't notice that Presley carried a woman's sweater. Their team won its first-round tourney game that Tuesday evening. Rae was asleep by the time Bob returned to Murdock Court.

At work Wednesday Bob lingered as long as he could at the Scotlan warehouse until it was time to catch his bus. He didn't know if he wanted to see Rae. Damn woman was making too much money for him now, and it didn't look good for him, but he felt he had to go home and clean the house and cook and make everything nice for Rae. He told himself that that was his job and he'd better hurry home to do it.

He was wearing her sweater again when she came in. She'd noticed the hangers in her closet slightly disarrayed. She'd seen the vacuum cleaner propped against a closet door and dust cloths strewn on a living room table. Cooking was his thing; the housecleaning puzzled her, as did his mood. For the past few days he had seemed totally detached.

In a phone conversation with Sue that Wednesday, Rae said, "He's not talking. There don't seem to be two of us in here. It's really strange; it's like he's abdicating something—being a husband or being married or something. It's almost like *I'm* the man."

"Well, damn it, talk to him about it," advised Sue.

"Well, damn it, I can't. I keep trying to sit down and tell him what I'm seeing. I want to tell him everything's OK, but I don't feel secure about talking. I don't know what to say or do. On the surface, I guess it seems OK," said Rae, "but underneath, well, I don't know. It really isn't. I could talk to him about ball and maybe perk him up, but I don't think I can. I've always been able to think of something to do to make things OK for us, but this time I don't know. I just don't know what's going on in his head. He's like a stranger."

The second-round tournament game in Vallejo was Thursday evening. Bob drove with Scotlan again. They talked ball, and Bob kidded Scotlan about loafing during warmups. "You got to do something besides just dunk the ball." He laughed. "You got to stop being lazy and really warm up."

During the drive on Interstate 80, Bob smoked dope. "I'm getting fired up for the big game," he claimed, and the two men laughed. "Be nice to win the championship here, huh?"

Scotlan thought their team was good enough to do just that. They won on Thursday, defeating a team featuring a onetime member of the New York Knicks of the NBA. They savored the victory in front of a 7-Eleven store in Vallejo—Scotlan quaffing a beer and Bob sipping on a bottle of orange juice.

"You played tonight the way you can play," said Scotlan. "You blocked shots, you rebounded great, you hooked real fine, you made the outlet passes. Everything you were supposed to do."

Bob could not sustain the high on Friday. Sure he had played well, yet what could come out of it? Just numbers and the praise of a few guys who were his friends and knew what he could do in ball anyway. Nobody who counted seemed to be aware of his abilities, and even if they were, they didn't have any interest in him. He was wasting his time—in ball, at Scotlan's. Filling days, that was all. He endured his shift mechanically, picked up his paycheck in early afternoon, reminding himself how little it seemed in comparison to Rae's salary, and headed to his bus stop at Alcatraz and Adeline.

It was early, not yet two, and Bob wasn't sure he wanted to go home this early, but there didn't seem much else to do; he thought he might as well catch the bus, do some housework, make dinner, and get himself together before Scotlan picked him up for that night's semifinal game in Vallejo. Another damn dumb game taking him nowhere, but still something to do.

Waddell Blackwell saw Bob at the bus stop as he drove by, heading home to Berkeley for lunch with a fellow named Fred. Waddell pulled over and asked his old college friend to join them. Bob agreed; it would kill some time.

At the Blackwell house, Waddell had trouble turning the key in the lock. He was fumbling with it when Bob said, "You can't trust women." Bob was angry. He was shouting. "Women can't be trusted."

Blackwell finally opened the door. He didn't know what to say to Bob. He looked at Fred as if to say, "Be cool."

Blackwell and Fred smoked a little grass, which Bob refused, and sat on the floor making small talk while Bob paced. The big man got angrier by the moment. "Women are terrible," he stormed. "They're taking over the world. All the bad things going on are their fault. Women are bad asses. They got to have control so they can keep you down. They don't want to mother you; they want to smother you."

Waddell still didn't know what to make of it, so he ignored it. But whenever Waddell and Fred were talking, Bob interrupted with his tirade. Blackwell had seen Bob angry many times. He knew better than to mess with the big man. He knew Bob couldn't let anything that seemed like a slur or a dig or an insult slide by. He also was aware that Bob and Rae's marriage was volatile, yet he'd never heard Bob talk this way about any woman. This wasn't Bob; this was incoherence.

Waddell considered calling the police. "The man needs help," he whispered to Fred.

He didn't believe Bob would hurt him, or Fred, or himself. But he wondered what would happen if a woman came into the house right now. What would happen if Bob went after Rae?

Waddell only hoped that the moment would pass, and within a few minutes it did. Bob finally stopped talking, and soon Blackwell dropped him back at the bus stop.

He understood Bob's frustration about ball; Waddell's sports career hadn't worked out either. It took him several years to emerge from his own disappointment—Bob wasn't the only guy who didn't make the NBA—but Blackwell was able to hide his depression in those years just after Cal. Bob often asked him, "How come you seem so up all the time?" And Waddell said it was only a front, that people wouldn't understand his feelings, that he knew he'd eventually come up. Bob never could fathom Waddell's ability to submerge feelings.

Now Blackwell wondered if Bob might not be better off going to Detroit. He knew Bob always had been happy in the company of his family; it might give him a lift. Bob's real problem, in Waddell's view, was an inability to get a decent job outside ball. Waddell believed the game was Bob's best hope—either that or go back to school, get a degree, and try for a good job in something else. Yet, even if Bob had a degree, Waddell wondered if anybody would hire him.

Blackwell himself was only six feet tall. He was average. He knew he survived by being average. But if a potential employer looked down a line of applicants and saw Bob there among a bunch of average-sized men, Presley would be snubbed. The average guy always makes it.

When he didn't hear from Bob for the next few weeks, Waddell presumed he'd gone to Detroit.

On the bus ride to East Oakland, Bob gripped the aluminum bar in front of his seat and held on tightly all the way. He squeezed and squeezed. At the shopping center bank near the house he cashed his check with a male teller. He didn't want any money from any woman anymore. Bob thought, You can't let them buy you because they'll own you, and if they own you, you got nothing left of yourself. What Bob had in his pocket at the moment was about $275 in cash. His. For two weeks of work. Janitor work. As he walked home, he wondered if Rae would be bringing her first paycheck from the new job. She better not. She better not come home, period.

The first thing he did at home was the breakfast dishes. He washed them, then threw them against the wall. Who the hell did she think she was? Then he went for the plants, all the plants. All the soil and all the foliage. Goddamn dirt. Is that all they think I am, goddamn dirt? Is that the way to treat a man, like dirt? What the hell do I count for around here? What the hell use am I? I'm no better than a goddamn woman, and they ain't worth shit.

When Rae came home, she stood for ten minutes at the door and watched. Bob did not acknowledge her presence. The only thing Rae knew for sure was that her husband had snapped. She told herself she was in a house with a man she had never seen before. She did not know what he was going to do. She was not about to ask.

Bob reached for a wooden shelf, tore it away from the wall, and banged it against the floor. For the first time in those ten minutes, he looked at Rae.

She understood. She knew she had to get out of there right now or be badly hurt. He was warning her he was going to hurt her unless she cleared out fast. She called Sue Steinpreis from a grocery store phone nearby.

"Do you have company? Can I come over?"

Sue asked who was calling. She didn't recognize Rae's voice. Sue had never heard Rae, or anyone, sound so terrified. A man at the store drove Rae to Sue's apartment near downtown Oakland.

At the same time Robert Scotlan telephoned Bob to tell him that night's game in Vallejo was off; their team had been disqualified for having too many semi-pros on the roster.

"That's good, man," said Bob, "because me and my wife are having some problems. I probably couldn't have made it to the game anyway."

Sue suggested Rae phone the police to help her get back into the house and get some clothing. Sue thought Rae should check on the dogs, too. She wondered if Bob had done anything to the dogs.

By nine thirty that evening, ten Oakland police officers were in the Murdock Court house looking for Bob.

When Rae telephoned the cops, it had taken her several minutes to persuade them that they would be dealing with a very large, very disturbed man. She knew that she alone couldn't help Bob now. He appeared to be beyond one-to-one assistance. She hoped the police could help Bob find help, that they could prevent him from whatever he intended. It was plain to Rae that he was bent on some form of destruction.

Rae was not the only one who phoned the police about Bob early that evening. Soon after she fled the house, Bob walked outside and saw the Lotts, a neighbor couple, in their driveway. The Lotts were in their sixties; the woman was ill and walked with crutches. As the Lotts merely stood there, stunned, Bob beat on the hood of their car with his fists and then grabbed the woman's crutches and threw them into the street. He screamed at them to get out of *his* driveway.

The two phone calls drew more than one police squad car; Rae, waiting nearby in a service station, counted five. But the officers did not find Bob in the house. Gone, too, was Ben, one of the German shepherds. When police assured her all was clear, Rae walked through the debris, gathered some clothing, and then returned to Sue's, taking along the other shepherd, Fritz, and her parakeet, Lucy. During the few moments it took to pick up her things, Rae had the eerie feeling that Bob was there watching her.

He was only a mile or so away; he had been running and running with the dog. He ignored the slash on his right hand; he'd cut himself when he ripped the shelf off the wall.

Early Saturday afternoon Rae asked the police to accompany her to the Murdock Court house again; she wanted to retrieve the rest of her things. As she approached the house with the officers, Bob was standing calmly in his front yard carrying two bags of groceries.

Rae was frightened. Sue, who had come with her, was too mad at the man to be frightened. From fifty yards away, they saw that Bob was bedraggled. Rae noticed his puffy hand and wondered if he'd been hammering away at the walls during the night. While the officers detained Bob outside, the women went into the house so that Rae could get what she needed. She was crying. As she walked back to the corner, Bob came over and said, very softly, "I'm sorry." He asked if she'd be coming back.

"I know you're sorry," she said, "but I can't take any more. I'm leaving." She handed him the key to the house.

As she walked away, she said to Sue, "I know it's over. So does he. For him now it's strictly ball. My place in his life is gone."

The police dispersed as Rae and Sue drove off. There was no arrest made because nobody had preferred charges.

Bob took the groceries into the house, made himself some lunch, and tried to sleep. He wanted a plan. He'd be okay without her, but he wanted a plan, and quickly, too.

The thing to do, he told himself, was go to Portland—not to wait for Hall to call Inman. Go and make the deal. But Hall had been straight; it might be wrong to mess on Hall now. At least let him know the plan. Tell him first; then do it.

This was Dale Hall's first free weekend since the WBA season had started in the fall; his first Saturday in several months with his wife, Jacquie, and his five kids. He was going to take her out to dinner tonight. She'd been patient with his basketball work, and helpful, too, even cooking and selling hot dogs at the games. He was changing clothes when the phone rang late in the afternoon. It was Bob Presley.

"I'm pretty uptight, coach," Bob explained. He hadn't meant to start that way. He wanted to get right down to business, to tell Hall he was heading for Portland, to move the plan right along.

"I did something stupid here at home. I messed up the place. I oughta leave town." He told Hall he felt lost without a game to play during the weekend. He said he was sorry the WBA season had ended so soon. Then he asked Hall if he had talked to anybody in Portland or to anybody else in the NBA.

"Sit tight, Bob," advised Hall. "The NBA season will be over pretty soon. Just sit tight. It's a little too soon for them to be thinking about prospects for next year."

"But what about Portland?"

"I talked to them earlier, and I'll talk to them again. But you've got to wait. You've got to take it easy." Dale wanted nothing more than for Bob to make the Trailblazers. If Portland signed Bob, it meant that a kid he coached had made the pros and he had helped him get there. Dale was pulling for that contract as much as Bob; Dale never kidded himself about his own ego.

"Take it easy," Hall said again to Bob, and hung up.

As he continued to dress, Dale told his wife that Bob sounded despondent. "I wish I were a better analyst," he said.

"Why don't you call him back?" Jacquie Hall asked.

In the second conversation, Bob still sounded urgent. "I'm really uptight," he said. "I don't know what to do."

"Wait another day," Dale replied. He didn't know what else to say to Bob. "Wait, and we'll see what we can work out. If you want me to, I'll come to Oakland now and we can talk."

"No that's OK," Presley assured him. "You don't have to bother."

"If you're sure, OK. But let's try to get together

tomorrow for a beer or something. I'll call you tomorrow." Hall hung up and thought about driving to Oakland to see Bob anyway, but he'd promised Jacquie
dinner. He couldn't disappoint her at the last minute;
that just wouldn't be right.

He telephoned Presley the next day, Sunday, but
there was no answer.

13

BOB WAS CONFUSED after his final conversation with Hall. He'd been told to wait, but why wait? What was there to wait for? If Portland didn't want him, he'd just as soon know now rather than wait another two, three weeks or maybe two, three months and waste time going to their rookie camp. He'd go see the man himself up there right now. He had to get this settled now.

Bob packed his athletic bag with his gym things, threw in his Muirs' jacket, grabbed his long leather coat because he remembered from Cal days it could be pretty cold up in Portland, and then locked the door at 22 Murdock Court. He stopped at a neighbor's to drop off the key. He gave Rae's office phone number to the neighbor and asked him to call her Monday and tell her he wasn't coming back.

He walked a few blocks until he found a taxi and told the driver to take him to San Francisco International Airport. Once over the Bay Bridge, Bob decided to stop and visit his cousin, Shelley Hart, in San Francisco. Shelley might have some news from Detroit.

They spoke for more than an hour about family, about old friends. Shelley was about fifteen years older. They'd grown up around the same Detroit neighborhood, knew the same people. Bob didn't see Shelley all that much here, and it was relaxing now to kick around old times. Bob told Shelley and Shelley's wife, Robbie, who was also from Detroit, that he might be going away for a while; up north, probably. Then he took a cab directly to the airport.

There was no flight to Portland for several hours. Bob didn't want to sit around the airport that long. He asked about flights to Seattle; at least he'd be up north, in a town he'd seen while playing for Cal, and then he could always rent a car and drive to Portland from Seattle. He didn't remember it being too far. Better than staying at the airport or going back home. Hell, he couldn't go back home anyway; no key. He only had to wait fifty-five minutes for a nonstop to Seattle.

By ten thirty he'd taken a cab downtown from Sea-Tac Airport, had some doughnuts, and checked into the Seattle YMCA. Before he went to sleep, he read a newspaper and noticed the SuperSonics would be playing in Seattle on Sunday against Phoenix.

He planned to work out in the Y during the day and then go to the game. Best thing to do was go early and try to talk to the SuperSonic people about a tryout. Thing to do was see Bill Russell, the Seattle coach and general manager. He knew some people Russell knew— Bob Bell and Bill Belford and all those people. He'd talk to Russell about a tryout. Or he might just walk out there and warm up on his own. SuperSonics tomorrow and then down to Portland on Monday to see the Trailblazers. This was working out just fine. His plan was a good one, and he was doing it on his own. He didn't need Rae or her money or anyone or anyone's help. Who'd ever helped him anyway?

His mind was so full of plans that it took several hours for Bob to drift into sleep. When he awakened, it was nearly noon. He went out for orange juice and fruit and then came back and worked out in the Y gym, practicing his left-handed hooks mostly. Must have thrown up a hundred of them. Russell would want to know if he could hook with either hand, so he'd show him. Then an hour of free throws and dunks and right-handed hooks and banging the ball against the boards so that he could rebound.

When he decided it was time to go back to his room and get dressed to go to the Seattle Center Coliseum, he realized he was alone in the gym. The ball he had checked out was old, but firm. Not a bad ball. Bob thought he might be able to use the ball, maybe practice with it in a park in Portland in case he couldn't find a gym down there. He glanced around, still saw no one, wrapped a towel around the ball, and took it with him, back to his room and out on the street as he walked to the arena dribbling on the sidewalk and bouncing the old ball off parked cars and the sides of buildings.

The Seattle-Phoenix game was due to start at seven. Bob arrived shortly after five and stood outside the players' entrance. As usual, there was a group of young blacks roaming nearby—asking for extra tickets and autographs.

"Who you, man?" said a kid of about twelve.

"A player, child. A superstar," boasted Presley.

"You new, man?"

"Sort of," admitted Bob. "New, and old."

"You got tickets?"

Bob hadn't bought his own yet. "C'mon, child," he

said to the kid. "We'll get us some tickets." The two
were followed to the ticket window by several other
youngsters. Bob bought seats for them all and gave his
first companion some money to buy everybody food.

Bob located the Sonics' dressing room, saw that no one
blocked the entrance, and walked in looking for Russell.
He asked the first player he spotted and was told Russell
would be around later.

Bob wasn't sure what to do now; it would be better
if he could talk to Russell early, right away. He saw
Spencer Haywood seated on a folding chair. Haywood:
from Pershing High, from Denver, and now the Sonics'
main man. Bob waved a friendly fist at Haywood and
wondered what to do next.

The team's trainer, Frank Furtado, was in an adjoin-
ing room taping several of the players; it was nearly an
hour and a half until game time.

"Some guy in the locker room looking for Russ," a
player told Furtado. "Check him out. Nobody seems to
know him."

Furtado walked over to Bob. "Can I help you with
something?" He didn't immediately notice that Bob
held a basketball under his left arm. What the trainer
did see were the skinned knuckles on the man's right
hand as Bob extended it, as if to say, assumed Furtado,
"You're the trainer, fix me up."

But all Bob did say was, "I need to talk to Russell."

"Well, he's not here yet. Best thing to do is just wait
for him outside in the hall. You can talk to him there.
You won't miss him if you just wait outside there because you'll be able to spot him when he comes in. Try
that. I can't guarantee he'll talk to you then, though,
because it might be too close to game time and he'll

need the time to talk to the team. But you can try."

"But I'm here to play for your team," Bob said.

The few players within earshot heard the comment and looked at each other in surprise. Furtado assumed from the man's size he was a player, but he had no idea who Bob was. The trainer wondered if the stranger might not have been picked up from another club in a deal he hadn't heard about, but that didn't seem possible: Furtado always knew about deals, about who was coming. He again asked Bob to wait outside the locker room and didn't see him again until halftime.

Bob waited at the locker room entrance for Russell. He wanted to stay with the players inside; it was comfortable being in there. But this was no time for a hassle; he didn't want to get his ass thrown out of the building before he could see Russell.

When he finally did spot the coach, Bob couldn't reach him in time. Russell breezed straight into the locker room.

Well, there was still the rest of the night. During the first half, Bob roamed around the arena, occasionally sitting in any empty seat, but most of the time just circling, thinking of what he was going to tell Russell when he reached him. Bob didn't notice people staring at him: a big man like that hauling around a basketball during a game.

A few minutes before the end of the half, Bob lingered in front of the locker room and then walked inside on the heels of the players. Furtado heard one of them ask, "Who *is* that dude?" and another say, "Some guy who played at the University of California." But he didn't hear a name mentioned. Then he saw Bob walk over to Russell and mutter something, only to have the coach say, "No way I can talk to you now."

Again Bob was shown to the door.

He considered leaving—the arena, the Y, the town—and flying back to Oakland. What the hell was he doing up here anyway? It wouldn't work out. Portland wouldn't work out. Why didn't they understand that he could *play* this game?

Bob found a seat and pondered his course. The second half began; he looked up to watch the action and set the ball down on an empty adjacent seat. He became absorbed in watching the game, particularly the big centers. He anticipated their moves. He knew how he'd react if he were out there.

Those centers are no damn good, he thought. Both these teams need a center. I could play for both these teams.

Tommy Burleson, Seattle's seven-foot-two center, was twenty-three years old, with a salary of more than $150,000 in this, his first, NBA season. Burleson was a white Carolina lad who appeared fragile, often uncoordinated, and, according to league appraisal, at least two or three years away from stardom in the pros. He considered himself privileged to be studying at the feet of Bill Russell. The coach had told Burleson, "A basketball player is like a pretty girl: you get pampered by coaches and everybody else. You're taken care of. Then you're left. The coaches leave you. Just like a pretty girl who's not pretty anymore."

Following the 102–96 loss to Phoenix, Burleson showered and wandered back into the locker room to dress. From the shower room alcove he could see the big black guy who'd been in the locker room before the game and again at halftime. Nobody seemed sure who he was—and here he was again, this time sitting in Burleson's cubicle. Bob was putting on Burleson's sneakers.

"I'm the new center on this team," said Presley.

"Hey, Burly," a player yelled to Tom, "just take your towel and go home. Your replacement's here." Several of the players laughed. Burleson was not amused.

"Take my shoes off," Burleson told Presley. Bob ignored him.

"Let it slide," advised the assistant coach, Bob Hopkins.

"I had a dream to come to Seattle," Bob said, still lacing the sneakers.

Burleson didn't know what to make of this. He asked Furtado to handle the situation.

Bob stood up and walked around in Burleson's sneakers for a few seconds as if modeling them. He said nothing, then sat back down and took them off. Furtado thought he'd let the guy be, let him wait for Russell.

Burleson dressed quickly. He and Slick Watts were the only players still in the locker room, the two of them, Furtado and his assistant, and Presley. As the two players headed for the door, Bob took his ball, the scuffed basketball, and softly shot it into a small rectangular wastebasket. Burleson and Watts heard him say, "Stay in there, you devil. Stay in there."

The two players walked out, but Bob lingered inside. Apparently Russell wouldn't be coming. Furtado didn't know whether to fetch a security guard or not. "I'm a little worried," he told his assistant. "There's just the two of us, and this guy is big. If he causes a disturbance, he's big enough that he could be a problem for us. He seems calm, but I don't know." The trainer decided to try talking to Presley.

"Did you get to see Russ?"

"Not yet."

"Well, listen, we have practice late tomorrow morning and that would probably be a good time to talk to him. We're closing up in here now, and Russ won't be around, so why don't you catch him here tomorrow?"

Bob glared at the wastebasket and walked out.

In the players' parking lot, Burleson and Watts talked briefly about the intruder and the old ball.

"Strange damn thing, huh?" said Burleson.

"Weird," agreed Watts. "Especially what he said."

From the arena back to the Y Bob had no sense of movement, of touching the pavement, of any noise around him, of the lights or the traffic or the few other pedestrians, of anything, of being. He wanted to think but couldn't. He was surprised he made it back to his room, to his bed. He did not undress. He stretched out, his feet dangling over the bed as they usually did in hotels, and was numb. He thought he might be hungry, couldn't remember when he'd last eaten or what it was he'd eaten. He awakened once, at near light, wondering where he was. It must have been a few hours later when he again awakened—the sun was sharing the room—to wonder who he was. He remembered something about a Monday morning practice, a basketball practice. See Bill Russell there. Talk to the man. He touched his clothing and wondered why he'd forgotten to bring a dress.

In mid-afternoon he packed, checked out, and walked to the bus station. There was business for him in Portland. He ate a burger, drank a Coke, reconstructed his plan, and boarded a Greyhound to Portland. He told himself he wasn't counting on anything happening for him in Seattle anyway. Portland was the place that wanted him, and now he was going there. He counted the money he had left, looked vacantly at the bleakness landscaping Interstate 5, and dozed off, trying to remember what he'd done with that old basketball.

The Greyhound driver at first thought Bob was sleeping. He remembered the big man was going to Portland, and when he didn't leave the bus, the driver figured he was dozing. The driver walked down the aisle, saw the large black man motionless in his seat, and worried about having to nudge someone so big. But as he stopped alongside Presley's seat, the driver saw that Bob actually was awake, head bent slightly forward but eyes opened.

"Portland, sir. You had a ticket to Portland."

Bob did not answer. Or move.

"I'm sorry, sir, but you're supposed to get off here." The driver hoped he wouldn't need help in dislodging this hulk.

"What do you want, man?" Bob lifted his head and stared at the driver.

"We're in Portland, sir."

"What's the problem?" The voice was very flat. The driver did not know what to make of the stare. The big man appeared to be lost or frightened. The driver wasn't sure what was going to happen here.

"Your ticket was only to Portland, sir. You'll have to get off."

"Right now?"

"Please, sir."

Bob stood, scrunched under the overhead rack, and walked up the aisle as the driver stepped aside.

"This your bag and coat, sir?"

"What?"

"This leather coat and sports bag."

"Oh, uh, yeah. Thanks. Did you say Portland?"

"Right, sir. Portland."

The driver called after Bob to ask him where he played basketball, but the big man didn't answer. The driver wondered if he might have heard of him so he could tell people that a famous basketball player had been on his bus.

Bob was not sure what time it was. He found a chair in the bus station but had to squeeze into it because a coin-operated TV set was attached. He dropped in two quarters but didn't watch.

A black about twenty years old sat two seats down. He nodded at Bob, who shrugged back.

Bob didn't know what he wanted to do right now. During the ride down he had thought about staying over in Portland tonight and then in the morning going over to the Trailblazer office to see this general manager Dale Hall had talked to him about. This Inman guy. Portland was having trouble with Bill Walton; they might want another center.

Bob couldn't remember why he hadn't been able to talk to Bill Russell in Seattle. He knew he'd seen Russell in the locker room. What had happened that they couldn't talk? Yes, the thing to do was stay here in Portland tonight and talk to Inman tomorrow. Maybe he should call Inman now, at home, and make some kind of appointment. No, he'd just go to the arena in the morning and see Inman. Just walk in and tell him that Portland's problems at center were all over.

Bob felt in his pocket for the money. About twenty dollars left. He could get a room here somewhere and then some breakfast and then see Inman. But then how would he make it home? Maybe Inman would sign him on the spot and give him plenty of money, or at least plane fare home.

He heard someone talking and did not realize the voice came from the television set on the seat. He thought the black kid next to him was speaking. He was very tired.

"You want something?"

"You talking to me, mister?"

"Yeah. Weren't you talking to me?"

"Uh, no. But I'll rap if that's what you want."

Maybe the kid knew where he could crash. "You got a place?" Bob asked.

"Sort of."

"Got room for me? Just one night. Just tonight."

The kid looked at Bob's legs stretching out from the seat. "You play ball, man?"

"Sure. And I sleep, too. You got room?"

"Who you play with?"

"Around California. Team in California, in San Francisco and around."

"The Warriors, man? What you doing here if you're with the Warriors?"

Bob unpeeled from the seat and walked to the restaurant counter. The kid called after him, "You still got time on the TV."

The girl at the counter was young and white. Maybe he could get lucky. It was late, and Bob thought she might be off soon. Work on it.

"Orange juice and something later," he said.

He told her he was in town to try out with the Trailblazers. He asked her all about Portland, about the spots. She was busy cleaning the milkshake machine and ignored him. He wanted to pull her over to him and just tell her to take him to her place. He was tired.

"Can we go to your place? Could you close up and could we go now?"

"My husband's coming at eleven o'clock," she said. "We can't go now, and we can't go later. So you just go away, you just clear out and stop screaming at me, mister."

How could he scream when he was so tired? "I really need to crash right away."

"You want I should call a cop, mister? You get away fast, or I will."

"C'mon, brother. Time to go." The black kid who had spoken with him earlier put his hand on Bob's leather coat. The kid was calm. "Just come with me, brother."

"Can I crash with you, man?" The kid told Bob he could if there was room, but there wasn't room, and he was sorry.

"They have a place up the hill here. The Contact Center. You go there—mostly white folks—but you go there and they'll get you a pad."

He pointed. He repeated the directions several times until Bob could say them back. He even walked along a few blocks and watched to make sure Bob headed up Morrison Street. The kid kept wondering who the big guy played for. Couldn't have been the Warriors.

The Portland Contact Center, a modest agency that provided counseling and a hot line and crash pads ("temporary housing referral services"), was in an old, three-story, unheated building at Sixteenth and Morrison. The Center served everything from understanding conversation to rock music. It had a few professional staff members but was usually manned, particularly at this hour on a Monday evening, by volunteers.

As he walked into the center, Bob didn't notice the announcements tacked to the double wooden doors at the top of the concrete steps. He just wanted to sleep.

Stan, a dark-haired office executive of thirty-eight, had been a volunteer at the center for a year. He was on the seven-to-midnight shift tonight. It had been quiet; already it was nearly ten thirty. As Bob came down the long, drafty hall, Stan was at his desk talking to another young man seeking a place to crash that night. Stan looked up at the imposing figure and nodded at Bob to sit down in an old, overstuffed chair. The center managed on tacky donated furniture, what there was of it.

Stan hoped he could find lodging for the kid at the desk. The list of potential crash pads was pretty slim. Eight or so. A few of the pad volunteers had been ripped off lately and dropped out. The crash houses were occupied mostly by young people; they trusted the center's judgment and were humane toward their overnight guests: a bed, perhaps a meal, with no questions asked.

Stan was on the phone talking to a pad volunteer. He looked up and saw Bob crumpling paper and tossing it— no, shooting it—into a wastebasket. Stan was struck by the man's size, but he couldn't get around to talking to him until he'd placed this first fellow, and that took about twenty minutes.

Bob sat quietly in the chair all that time. Maybe they'll let me crash right here, he thought. He saw a couch against the wall on the left. The couch would be fine. He could sleep right there and then in the morning walk down and see Inman at the arena.

Stan came over, introduced himself, shook hands, and escorted Bob to the chair just vacated by the other man. His first thought was that this man must be connected with pro basketball. But if he was, what was he doing here?

"How come you're in Portland?"

"For ball," Bob answered. "I play ball."

"Are you going to play here?"

"I play in California, and I was in Seattle over the weekend, and now I'm here. I came here from Seattle, but I may go back to California."

Stan was accustomed to disjointed conversations. There was no rush; no one else was waiting. The big man seemed OK; a little rambling, but OK.

"I'm just traveling around," Bob explained. "There's a few people here I can see, but nobody in particular, and I just might not bother seeing anybody. I live in California, in Oakland. I think I'm breaking up with my wife, so I'm just moving around a little. Seattle, here, different places. Traveling."

Bob rambled on for ten minutes. Stan did not interrupt, feeling that Bob might make a point or ask for something.

Bob alternately sat at the desk and paced. He told Stan he'd gone to the University of California in Berkeley and played ball there. He didn't know what was going to happen with his marriage. He was playing ball and wanted to keep playing ball. And he spoke some more about going to Seattle and coming to Portland on his way back to Oakland.

Stan asked if he had money, and Presley pulled the bills out of his pocket, along with a stick of Doublemint. Stan had the impression that all the big man wanted to do was talk a few minutes.

"Is there anything in particular I can do for you?" Stan finally asked.

"I'm tired. I need to crash somewhere. I got this money, but I'll need it to move on tomorrow. I'm thinking of going home. I don't know if I will, but I'm thinking about it."

"You want a place to stay tonight then?"

"Please," said Presley.

Stan excused himself for a moment, and Bob went back to the big chair. Stan checked the remaining names on the list of crash pad volunteers. Only a couple left. He hoped he could connect, but now it was really late. He tried Mike Shank on the Northeast Side, on Crane Street. There was a notation Shank worked nights, but perhaps he was off or someone else in the home would be willing to let Bob come over. But Shank did have the night off. Stan explained to him the guest was black and quite big. "The only reason I'm telling you this now," explained Stan, "is that I don't want you to be shocked when you see this imposing figure walking up to your door." Shank said to send him over; it would be OK.

Stan gave Bob directions to the bus, and Presley walked back down Morrison. He wondered if he wanted to spend the night with strangers. Maybe he should go back to the Greyhound station and ask about a bus to Oakland. Maybe he could walk to the freeway and thumb.

But then there was Inman and the Trailblazers. Inman might want him. He could work out for Inman in the morning. A little shoot-around. He would show him. Inman would have to take him because he could do the job. Russell should have talked to him. Why wouldn't Russell talk to him? Russell could have checked him out with Belford. Belford would have told Russell, but Russell paid him no attention. That was wrong. He could go to Seattle and try to see Russell again. Maybe he could grab a bus back up there tonight. Hell, he could afford the fare to Seattle better than the fare to Oakland. Probably nowhere near enough to go to Oakland anyway. Seattle was just up the road. Well, that's what he'd do if Inman turned him down. See Inman, then try Russell again. That's what he'd do.

At the corner of Fifth and Morrison, Bob asked directions to the city bus stop. A man crossing the street pointed him a block to the right, toward Yamhill. "Right in front of the Pioneer Federal Courthouse," the man told him. Bob remembered now: the Number 8 Irvington in front of the federal courthouse. He remembered too that he had the name and address of the crash pad people in a pocket of his leather coat. He had wrapped the piece of paper with the address around the thirty-five cents he'd need for the bus fare.

He hoped there'd be no hassle from these people. He was too tired for hassle. He wanted to sleep.

Mike Shank was twenty-four years old and a night clerk at the main post office. He was of medium height, thin, with red hair. He rented this house on Crane Street: a two-story gray stucco with aluminum siding. Sufficient room for his tiny, twenty-three-year-old wife, Jan, and their two-year-old daughter, Madeline. Often Mike's younger brother, Larry, who was twenty-two and a waiter, stayed with them. Larry thought Mike's services as a crash pad host rather amusing; he couldn't understand this business of permitting strangers to spend a night in your home.

After Stan telephoned from the crisis center, Mike told Larry there would be a tall black man coming over. Larry smiled at his brother's benevolent bent; in a few minutes Bob arrived. Mike and Jan were upstairs.

Bob shook hands with the young man and was shown into the living room. "Sit anywhere you want," Larry said, so Bob flopped onto an orange beanbag chair on the floor. Larry sat alongside in a canvas director's chair and wondered what to talk about until Mike and Jan came down.

Bob appreciated the silence. It felt good just to sit. He was so tired. He hoped they would let him sleep right here and not question him about anything. They would want to know where he was from and what was he doing in Portland and did he have family, and he didn't want to think about those things.

He knew he was working hard to block out Rae, where she might be now or if he would ever see her again or if he wanted to or if she wanted to see him. This time it was probably finally over. This time would end it, and she'd be better off and he'd be better off. She didn't need him. She was doing all right and she would keep doing all right. Who the shit needed him? The world's tallest janitor.

The thing to do was go to Detroit, go home, start something new, be your own man. That would be right. It would be better in Detroit. Maybe the Pistons would look at him. The Pistons had a black coach. But, hell, they had their big man there. Lanier. They wouldn't want to look at him; they didn't need him. Maybe going back to Seattle made more sense. This time, maybe, Russell would talk to him. Why hadn't Russell talked to him Sunday? What went wrong Sunday? What did he do?

Jan came downstairs, heard no conversation, and wondered what Larry and the big man were doing. She thought she heard someone crying and for a moment wondered if Madeline had awakened. But the sounds were from the beanbag chair. Bob was sobbing, softly but audibly. Larry glanced at Jan and shrugged his shoulders. Bob didn't notice the woman. He folded his hands on his lap, let his head fall forward, and wept.

"It's OK," Larry said. "You're with friends. You'll get a good night's sleep, and it'll be OK."

Jan quietly introduced herself. "Maybe you'd like something to eat," she suggested. "A cup of coffee or something." Crashers usually were hungry, Jan knew. Often too hungry.

Bob shook his head no. Right now he didn't need a woman telling him what to do. Or was this a woman? Looked more like a little girl.

Jan was four feet, eight inches tall.

"It's no bother," she said. "How about a sandwich?"

Bob realized he was crying. Why was he crying? How long had he been crying? When was the last time he cried? He couldn't remember if he'd cried in Seattle. Was he really crying?

"Jan's a good cook," said Larry. "She can put together a real good sandwich quick. Might be a good idea to eat something." Larry didn't know what else to say, and Jan went upstairs to fetch Mike, who'd been napping.

"It can't be that bad," Larry prompted. "You're probably just tired. You'll get some sleep—this is a nice quiet place—and you'll feel better." He was running out of consoling conversation when Mike came down and introduced himself. Bob unfolded his hands and waved. He daubed at his eyes with a sleeve.

"Want to talk about it?" asked Mike. "You can talk to us if you want. We're just people here. We're used to listening."

Bob sensed the redheaded guy was OK. Nice, quiet voice. No hassle. Talk to him. Talk for a while. Don't cry.

"You look like a guy who used to sit next to me in

class in Berkeley," Bob said. "Smart cat. Smart little white cat. Wonder what happened to him. Don't even remember his name. Didn't say much but always got A's. That was in Berkeley, at Cal. I live in Oakland now. Oakland, California, with my old girlfriend, my wife. Except now I'm the wife." He heard himself weeping again.

Larry went upstairs with a sense of relief. Jan came down to keep Mike company. She listened to Bob ramble, about college and basketball and his wife. She sat on the floor next to Mike and listened. It was best to listen.

"She threw me out," Bob explained. "My girlfriend threw me out. My wife. Ripped off my manhood and threw me out. That's what she did to me. No more man, no more nothing. Then in Seattle they wouldn't listen. My neighbors wouldn't listen there in the driveway either. Trouble with the neighbors after she threw me out and ripped me off. But I'm going to play ball. You'll see. I'll play. You'll see. If they give me the right money, I'll play. I'm ready. I've been playing a lot. I'm in shape, and if they pay me, I'll play for them. If it's not enough, I won't. I'm not going to give it away. If I had money now, I'd quit my job and get in real shape and then they'd sign me. For big money. See that canvas chair, there? Friend of mine had a chair like that in Berkeley, in his place. I know that chair. I've been in that chair. But what good is a chair? What good is anything? Ball's no good. Nothing's good. You see what I mean?"

Mike and Jan listened for more than an hour. When Bob paused, they asked questions, general questions: how long had he been married, where had he come from, what kind of work did he do, what were his plans. When he said his masculinity was "ripped off," Jan said, "No one can take your manhood away, Bob."

They sought to console, to try to understand. But it was hard. Bob looked at the Shanks' fireplace and talked about a fireplace he'd had somewhere; then he talked about a similar living room he'd seen, even about another beanbag chair, or end table. Everything seemed to represent something to him, and Mike and Jan had no idea what Bob was driving at. They recognized Presley's depression, but as midnight passed, his persistent rambling muddied their attempt at compassion. They wanted to soothe the big man, but they simply did not know what to say. And when they did speak, he paid no attention.

At one point, Jan excused herself and went upstairs hoping to sleep. But she couldn't. She lay awake thinking about the big man, hearing his low tones, hearing Mike's digressions and questions, wondering how long this would go on. After a half hour, she rejoined the two men in the living room.

Bob heard his voice growing louder. He had to tell these people. He had to concentrate and tell them good. Even if he had to shout, he would make them realize how he'd been messed with.

"I'm going to the Trailblazers," he said. "Then I'm going to Seattle. Or I'll go home to Oakland. But I know it won't work out. Not here and not there. But I've got to go. I'm a woman now and I've got to go. I do dishes. I clean house. I'm a housewife, a woman. A woman's got to go. I guess I'll hitchhike. No money to travel. So I'll just thumb. There's always people thumbing in Berkeley. They go down University Avenue to a couple of blocks from the freeway, and they thumb because the freeway goes everywhere. They have no money either. They're not going anywhere either. I'll go home and try to work things out. I'll hitchhike and put it together again with my woman, with the neighbors. Then I can play ball."

Mike tried to sort it out. He had the man's name. He knew he was married—the girlfriend and the wife were the same woman from what he could fathom. He knew Presley had played ball at Cal in Berkeley because the name seemed to be vaguely familiar; anyway the man had to have played basketball somewhere. Mike was not clear on the Seattle references, or on the difficulty with the neighbors, or on this talk of a tryout with the Trailblazers. He didn't know whether Bob had any money, but his notion was that the man wouldn't be there if he did. Mike thought about giving Bob a few bucks but wondered if he'd use it to get to Oakland. Presley didn't know what he wanted to do. Mike felt going home might be the best move for him. If he could get Bob to sleep, he would persuade him in the morning to go home. That was Mike's aim; he'd work at that.

"How about crashing?" Mike asked.

"No, you go on. Don't worry about me. There's nothing left to worry about. You just go up, and I'll be OK here. I've been in a room like this before; I know this place. We can keep talking here. I'd rather talk than sleep. But if you're tired, you go on upstairs. No need to talk if you're tired."

At about two thirty, Mike and Jan left the room. Jan had a doctor's appointment early in the morning. They had to get some sleep, and they thought that with nobody to talk to Bob might finally sleep, too.

In their bedroom they talked quietly about him. "I can't understand the fatalism," Mike said. "None of it makes any sense. Maybe we should call somebody, some agency, in the morning. The guy needs help. I don't think there's anything we can do here tonight. Let's see how he is in the morning and see what they suggest."

Jan was disturbed by Bob's behavior. The man sounded suicidal. She tried to sleep. She heard Bob walking around heavily downstairs. She heard him in the kitchen. It sounded as if he were sweeping the kitchen floor. Seemed strange, but that's what it sounded like.

Bob propped the broom against the kitchen table. There, the floor was done. Now he'd do the dishes for these people. And maybe when he cleaned up the kitchen, he could make everybody a meal.

But maybe he was a problem for them. Maybe he should go. He'd kept them up; he'd cried; he'd been loud. He was sorry. He'd go and tell them he was sorry for bringing them trouble. He was big trouble, and they didn't have any of this coming. He should tell them.

Jan heard his large footsteps on the staircase. She nudged Mike, but he wasn't sleeping either.

"He wants us for something," Mike said.

"Hey, Mike," Bob called from the top of the stairs. "Hey, man, forgive me, will you, man? Will you forgive me? Please, man?"

Mike got up and walked to the bedroom door and said, "Sure, Bob. It's OK. C'mon downstairs and let's talk some more."

Jan went down with them. She smelled something burning and went to the kitchen and saw an empty pot on a lighted electric burner.

"I'll get it," Bob said. "I washed it, and I was drying it on your stove. I'll get it. That's my job."

Before he went to the kitchen, Bob walked to the banister and grabbed a black, full-length skirt Jan had put there. "Is this for me?" he asked her. She was too stunned to answer.

Bob wrapped her elastic-waisted skirt around his belt line and went into the kitchen. He took the pot off the burner, turned off the burner, picked up the broom, and swept the floor.

"I'm a woman," he said. "I do this."

Then he went to the sink and began washing dishes. He had not taken off the skirt. He appeared to be talking to the sink. "I can see it all now," Bob said flatly. "Looks like the end of the road. I can't be forgiven. This is the end."

Jan was frightened. She wanted to ask the man what he was going to do. She whispered to Mike that she thought Bob was talking suicide. Mike softly said no; he didn't think so.

They agreed Bob didn't seem to be on drugs. "He's speeding, but he's clean," Mike whispered.

He suggested she go back to bed, that he'd stick it out. Mike thought Bob might want to sleep after finishing in the kitchen. It was well past 3:00 A.M.

Back in the living room, Bob took off the skirt and wrapped his long leather coat around him. He paced the room without speaking for several minutes. Mike wondered if the big man might finally be spent.

"Why don't we try and catch some sack time, Bob? It's almost morning, and we all have to get away early. OK?"

Bob stopped and looked pleadingly at Mike. "Please don't leave me alone," he said. "Please."

"Sure. Let me just get a bag and bring it down here. I'll stay right here with you. Don't worry."

"You'll come right back?"

"Sure, Bob. Right away."

Bob sat down on the beanbag chair again, and Mike spread his sleeping bag on the living room floor and waited for Bob to talk. But the big man was silent. All he did was pop up and down. He walked around, often with his eyes closed, bumping into tables and chairs.

Jan listened from the bedroom and worried about Mike.

Mike fought sleep. It was comfortable in the bag, he was exhausted; yet he was fearful of dozing. He didn't think Bob would hurt them or himself, but he couldn't be sure. He thought about the possibility of Bob grabbing a knife in the kitchen.

Bob nudged the man in the bag. The man was sleeping, and Bob felt alone. He didn't want the man to sleep. "Talk to me, Mike. Talk to me."

Shank felt himself being poked by a leg.

"The nights are bad for me," Bob explained. "The nights are the worst. I'm frightened."

"There's nothing to be frightened about here," Mike said. "It's nearly morning. The dark's nearly gone. Hang in, Bob. Get some sleep. C'mon."

Mike drifted in and out of sleep. Each time he awakened, he saw that Bob was also awake—either walking around the room or sitting in the beanbag.

Bob talked to himself. Over and over, about the same things: what to do, where to go.

No destination was important. He couldn't play ball in Seattle, or in Portland, or even back home. The seasons were all over everywhere. Teams in the playoffs wouldn't be giving tryouts and teams not in the playoffs wouldn't care until training camp time. No more ball for now, except in the parks or gyms, and what the hell did those places mean anymore anyway? Just grown guys hanging around with nothing to do but play like kids. Wasn't worth anything; waste of time. No sense going back out to those places. Or anywhere. Bob wondered if Shank had a stereo and some jazz. Music would make him fall asleep.

By seven o'clock everybody in the house was awake and in the kitchen. Jan made Bob tea and toast. He was subdued. He told Mike and Jan and Larry he still didn't know where he wanted to go. The two men suggested he'd be better off heading for Oakland.

"But what shoes will I wear?" Bob asked.

"Doesn't matter," said Larry. "Just go home and things'll work out." Mike agreed.

"I don't know if I want to hitchhike," Bob said. "I'm afraid to hitchhike. I don't know what to do."

Mike and Larry kept after him about returning home. They said it was the best alternative. They said he'd have no problems thumbing and not to worry, that there was nothing to be afraid of on the road.

Bob went upstairs to the bathroom. Jan wondered whether he should be alone. Mike said to wait and see.

"Best thing to do," Bob said when he returned to the kitchen, "is to get together with my wife, with Rae. That's what I know I should do."

"That's what we think, too," agreed Mike.

"But I don't know." Bob hesitated. "I don't know if she'd accept me. I'm not worthy of her anymore. I hit her. I hit my neighbors. I'm not worthy. How can I go back if I'm not worthy? The thing to do is go back up to Seattle. Anywhere but Oakland. Nobody will take me back in Oakland."

"Listen, Bob, why don't you just think about it, about going home?" said Mike.

Larry nodded. "We're going near the freeway. We'll drop you right there, and all you have to do is put out your thumb and head south, for home. It'll be easy. The best thing for you to do. Believe me, Bob."

"I would like to see my dogs again. I really would. But I just don't know."

"Forget what happened before you came up here," urged Mike. "Life goes on. You just go home and things will be all right."

Bob nodded. The Shanks believed they finally had convinced him to return home. He was gracious and coherent during the balance of breakfast, and at eight thirty they all left the house in Mike's car.

As they drove toward the freeway, Bob thanked them all. "I won't be taking up any more of your time," he said. Mike repeated directions to Oakland on Interstate 5, and Bob said, "Best thing to do is hitch home."

But he never told the Shanks that he was going to Oakland. He got out of the car at Alberta Street, just off the freeway. "Just go down there and you can get a ride." Mike pointed. "If things don't work out, go back to the Contact Center. They'll help you."

For an instant Bob seemed hesitant to walk away from the car. Then he said, "I'll hitchhike. That's what I'll do."

That afternoon, Mike Shank drove to the Contact Center and told a volunteer there to take his name off the crash pad list. He suggested that the center screen crashers more thoroughly. If Presley showed up at the center again in the next few days, Mike urged that they direct him to a self-help agency. But he was certain that Bob was on his way to Oakland.

Epilogue

LATE ON THE MORNING of Tuesday, March 25, 1975, Lewis W. Rose saw what appeared to be a small suitcase on a traffic island at the Portland intersection of Water Street and Hawthorne. He picked it up and patted it and was convinced it was filled with clothing. Rose didn't see anyone nearby, so he turned the bag over to the Portland police.

Inside they found a pair of size 13 Converse sneakers, a pair of tan laced boots of the same size, and a gold-and-blue athletic jacket with an oak tree logo stitched on. Also sewed onto the jacket were the words *Martinez* and *Bob.*

Officers determined that the bag cost eight dollars, but they didn't know who owned it. They decided to store it in the property room at police headquarters. On May 11 they learned the identity of the bag's owner.

Early that morning the tug U.S. *Lewiston* was passing down the Willamette River through the heart of Portland. In the near light a crewman on the *Lewiston* saw a large object bobbing along the riverbank between the Morrison and Hawthorne bridges near the foot of Southwest Yamhill Street. The *Lewiston* was not close enough for the crewmen to identify the object; he thought it looked like a body.

His sighting was radioed from the *Lewiston* to the bridge tender on the Hawthorne, who then called the fire department boat station below the east side of the bridge. The fire boat, the red-and-white *Karl Prehn*, clipped across the Willamette with its crew of Lieutenant Al Carocci, Richard Meyer, and Robert Burr. By 6:30 A.M. the *Karl Prehn* had moved alongside the body of a man Carocci guessed to be at least seven feet tall. All three of the firemen agreed that the body, because of its size and state of decomposition, would be difficult to pull out of the water. Once they did remove the body, the firemen were unable to fit it in the black rubber bag they stowed on the boat. The bag stretched only six feet. Finally, by not zipping up the bag, they did what had to be done.

Carocci radioed the Portland Fire Department dispatcher and asked him to notify the coroner's office. By 7:00 A.M. the coroner's wagon arrived at the fire boat station and picked up the unidentified floater.

Oregon State medical examiner Dr. William Brady did his work with the floater that afternoon. In his report he noted that the victim was wearing blue trousers, a blue long-sleeved cotton sweater with white and brown stripes, white sweat socks, and a pair of Converse tennis shoes.

The pockets of the blue trousers contained nineteen dollars in bills and sixty-five cents in change, a book of matches, a seven-stick pack of Doublemint gum containing one stick, a ticket stub to the Seattle SuperSonics basketball game of March 23, a receipt from the Seattle

YMCA, a fragment of a Seattle-to-Portland Greyhound Bus ticket, a small piece of paper—apparently ripped out of an address book—on which was written the address and phone number in Martinez, California, for a Dale Hall, and, finally, a small scrap of paper on which had been penciled the words "Need new address."

Doctor Brady ruled the cause of death as asphyxia by drowning and said there were no apparent injuries. He was unable to determine how long the body had been in the Willamette or how it got there.

Within a few hours, Portland police reached Hall in Martinez. On the basis of their conversation with him and eventual fingerprint identification and confirmation from the police department in Berkeley, California, the police in Portland were able to identify the floater as Robert Nathaniel Presley, whose twenty-ninth birthday had been on April 30 and who was six feet, eleven and one-half inches tall and 240 pounds, and who, from what the Portland police could determine, was a basketball player.

A reporter from the *Oregon Journal* asked a homicide inspector if the big man might have died for reasons other than suicide. "I don't think it's very likely," said the inspector, "that somebody picked up a man that size and just threw him into the river."

Within a few hours the story was on the radio and in the early edition of the *Oregonian*. Michael E. Shank read about it and called Portland police to tell them he believed the dead man was the same one who spent a night in his house in late March.

After a series of telephone calls to Oakland, the Portland police reached Rae at a house she'd rented in Berkeley two weeks previously.

McLister Presley came to Portland from Detroit to

claim his brother's body and arrange for its shipment to Detroit for services. Rae went directly to Detroit.

The funeral expenses included a cost the Presleys didn't anticipate: because caskets are only six feet, six inches long, a special casket had to be ordered for Bob at the cost of an extra twenty dollars an inch.

AUTHOR'S NOTES

THIS PROJECT began in late 1975 as a three-part series in San Francisco's fine *City Sports* magazine and fell into place as a biography with the extremely patient and skillful guidance of Gene Stone, the second-best editor I've had in twenty-five years of typing for money. My best editor is my wife, Gloria Sumner-Michelson, who has a greater eye for reality and clarity, and for life, than any grammarian. This book is dedicated to her.

Actual names are used in every major element of this story except one: the woman I call Adriana Wheeler agreed to be interviewed only if given an alias. There are, however, several fictionalized fringe characters employed for reasons of background and continuity: the two players on Presley's first bus trip west; people in the Portland bus station; the Seattle-Portland bus driver.

Presley's walk toward death in Portland is reasoned conjecture. There is no way to be positive about his actions and movements between the time the Shank family dropped him off near Interstate 5 and the discovery

247

of his equipment bag near the bridge. I walked several routes between those two points and ended up with what I can only hope is decent guesswork. Also, there is no conclusive evidence that Presley jumped from the Hawthorne and not another bridge; again, the proximity of his bag to the Hawthorne led me to that probability.

Some people who knew Bob Presley (I never met him or saw him play) believe, even now, that he was killed. But evidence—from the police, the coroner, the Shank family—inevitably leads one to conclude suicide.

Mill Valley, California   Herb Michelson